THE EMPIRE EXHIBITION OF 1938

The Empire Exhibition of 1938
THE LAST DURBAR

Bob Crampsey

MAINSTREAM PUBLISHING

Copyright © Bob Crampsey, 1988

All rights reserved
First published in Great Britain in 1988 by
MAINSTREAM PUBLISHING COMPANY (EDINBURGH) LTD
7 Albany Street
Edinburgh EH1 3UG
ISBN 1-85158-122 (cloth) 7

No part of this book may be reproduced or transmitted in any form or by any other means without the permission in writing from the publisher, except by a reviewer who wishes to quote brief passages in connection with a review written for insertion in a magazine, newspaper or broadcast.

British Library Cataloguing in Publication Data

Crampsey, Robert A. (Robert Anthony), 1930-
   The Empire Exhibition of 1938.
   1. Scotland. Strathclyde Region. Glasgow.
   Exhibitions: British Empire Exhibition
   (1938: Glasgow, Scotland)
   I. Title
   607′.34′41443

   ISBN 1-85158-122-7

Typeset in Goudy in 11 on 13pt
by Blackpool Typesetting Services Ltd, Blackpool, Lancashire
Printed in Great Britain
by Butler and Tanner Ltd, Frome, Somerset

CONTENTS

Acknowledgements		7
Foreword	The Great Design	9
Chapter One	One of the Thirteen Million	13
Chapter Two	Previous Experiences	27
Chapter Three	The Idea Takes Shape	39
Chapter Four	Overture and Beginners	53
Chapter Five	Off and Running – Early Days and Attitudes	65
Chapter Six	Mr Butlin's Pleasure Dome	83
Chapter Seven	Sport at the Empire Exhibition	93
Chapter Eight	Ordinary and Distinguished Visitors	105
Chapter Nine	That's Entertainment	115
Chapter Ten	How the Future Might have Looked	127
Chapter Eleven	September (And October) In the Rain	141
Chapter Twelve	Look on My Works Ye Mighty and Despair	151

ACKNOWLEDGEMENTS

Many people helped me in the preparation of this book. I should like to thank most particularly George Outram and Company Limited for allowing me access to their unparallelled collection of photographs of the Exhibition. Stanley K. Hunter was good enough to show his unrivalled collection of artefacts and made many helpful suggestions regarding the relation of the 1938 Exhibition to Glasgow Exhibitions as a whole. Gordon Stevenson also provided invaluable photographic material and I owe him my sincere thanks.

Charles A. Oakley was particularly generous in making himself available for interview on his part in running the Exhibition and for the point of view of a working journalist I am especially obligated to that most knowledgeable of Glaswegians, Jack House. The staff of the Mitchell Library were, as ever, unfailingly courteous and imaginative in their help and lastly, I gladly recognise the help of dozens of Scots who through their personal recollections of Bellahouston in 1938 made the Empire Exhibition come alive again for me.

FOREWORD
THE GREAT DESIGN

IT was the last large-scale appeal to an Imperial destiny. It was the last chance to glimpse what might have been the pattern of the peaceful 1940s. Here in Scotland, on the one site at Bellahouston Park, were built the flat-roofed ship's bridge pavilions which would never be transmuted to commercial structures. Here were concentrated the ideas which an imminent war would stifle, accelerate or change radically.

The venue and timing were deliberate. Central Scotland was emerging slowly from the horrendous unemployment of the early 1930s. Cecil Weir, one of the prime movers behind the Exhibition, later said: "The timing of the Exhibition was fortunate. Trade and industry were emerging from quiet and depressed times."

This is a remarkable piece of understatement, akin to describing the Battle of the Somme as a skirmish. Scotland had in the early Thirties almost half a million men out of work. Many were skilled men who had not been in work for as long as three years and who would without any sense of irony describe themselves as "idle", although almost every waking hour was spent tramping the streets on the off-chance that somewhere someone might be taking on labour.

The 1930s were stark enough in all conscience but they were never as unremittingly gloomy, even in the industrial West of Scotland, as subsequent legend has painted them. Films of the enormous crowds which attended football matches in Glasgow in those days (attendances over 120,000 were commonplace) show clearly that the bulk of the spectators were respectably if not always well-dressed and crowds of such magnitude were overwhelmingly working-class. The development of Association Football and the advent of talking pictures had brought cheap entertainment within the reach of all though the "movies", still a fairly daring word in 1938, would inevitably lead to the partial Americanisation of Britain in speech patterns and in aspirations.

For those in work, and they formed the great bulk of those who would attend the Exhibition, the late 1930s were oddly enough a time of comparative prosperity. There was no inflation, indeed the pound was worth more in 1938 than it had been in 1918 and there was an abundance of attractive factored property in such districts as Hyndland on the north side of the city and Pollokshields and Mount Florida on the south side. It was a buyer's market and it was by no means unheard of for a factor to clinch a tenancy by offering to paint and paper a flat without any payment being required. For anyone whose ambitions stretched a little further the expenditure of £350 would secure a bungalow in the fast-developing district of Newton Mearns.

It is a great mistake, though a common one, to think of the Glasgow of the early 20th century as an unrelieved industrial hell-hole. J. R. Allan in the chapter *Sketches for a Portrait of Glasgow* which he contributed to the book which he himself edited – *Scotland 1938* – saw this clearly with the cold and objective eye of an Aberdonian who had come to the warm, muggy south-western city: "Wherever there is great poverty there is usually great wealth and Glasgow has many fine houses founded upon the heartening Five Per Cents. Time was when anybody with a little capital could make a handsome competence in the town. Shipbuilding, shipowning, ironfounding, coalmining, importing, exporting, speculating – all these like horns of plenty showered their profits on Glasgow." Later in the chapter he touches on what he considered to be the real wealth of the city: "The town is dreadful in many ways. It is ugly in itself and too many people must live in a way that denies expression to the best qualities within them. But the life of the people has a richness, a warmth and a humour such as you do not find in any other part of Scotland and which, if it were allowed a free expression might transform Glasgow into a very wonderful town."

Even as the Exhibition was in preparation there were moves to extend the concept of paid holidays to manual workers. Until this came to pass few if any of the heavy industrial workers could afford extended holidays but even for them country parks were at the end of a twopenny ride on the Corporation tramcars which ran a good 15 miles in east-west directions from the city centre. The major

THE GREAT DESIGN

FINISHING TOUCHES. *The tri-towered building in the centre is the ICI Pavilion, the three towers representing air, fire and water.*

diseases, diphtheria, cholera, typhoid, had been overcome although there would be one last counter-attack from the white plague, tuberculosis. The chimney stalks still belched brown and yellow smoke but the new schools were lighter and airier.

By 1938 things were definitely on the turn. The *Queen Mary* had been launched, fitted out, sent to sea – the symbolism was far more important than the actuality. The Coronation of a King, George VI, who had come to the throne in circumstances which guaranteed him the sympathy of his subjects and of his Queen, Elizabeth, who had the affection of her fellow Scots, had also seemed to indicate that better days might just lie ahead. For the six months between May and October 1938 the wealth and tradition of the Empire was distilled in this Exhibition.

THE EMPIRE EXHIBITION OF 1938

It was important too that Scottish national sentiment, admirable in itself, should not be allowed to become Scottish Nationalist sentiment. There had been a couple of faint indications of the possibility of this. Of the major Scottish newspapers the *Glasgow Bulletin* was thought to be not ill-disposed to the Nationalist ideas and Compton Mackenzie, the author, had won a great deal of support when standing successfully as a Scottish Nationalist for the Rectorship of Glasgow University some seven years before.

The executive committee of the Exhibition consisted of prominent Scots industrialists such as the shipbuilder Sir James Lithgow, the engineer Cecil Weir and Sir Steven Bilsland. The patrons were aristocratic – indeed the list of Vice-Presidents is simply the Scots Peerage at Public Service. Five Dukes, three Marquesses and nine Earls were weighty guarantees of confidence. Another Earl, he of Elgin and Kincardine, was President of the enterprise.

The objects of the Exhibition were five in number and were set forth with gratifying clarity:

(1) To illustrate the progress of the British Empire at home and overseas.
(2) To show the resources and potentialities of the United Kingdom and Empire Overseas to the new generations.
(3) To stimulate Scottish work and production and to direct attention to Scotland's historical and scenic attractions.
(4) To foster Empire trade and a closer friendship among the peoples of the British Commonwealth of Nations.
(5) To emphasise to the world the peaceful aspirations of the peoples of the British Empire.

The phrase "Commonwealth of Nations" was used but there was no shrinking from the more robust words "Empire" and "Imperial". In his message for the opening of the Exhibition, the Prime Minister, Mr. Neville Chamberlain, said: "Scotland has in the past made a notable contribution to Imperial development. In her present effort I see an earnest of her resolve to add to that contribution."

Against this background, therefore, the Empire Exhibition of 1938 was held with all the confidence and sense of destiny of an organisation which covered one-quarter of the world's surface and on which, as every schoolboy and schoolgirl knew, the sun never set.

CHAPTER ONE
ONE OF THE THIRTEEN MILLION

ON a sunny early Spring day in March 1938 I sat on a grassy slope in Mosspark and looked down on the great work which was taking shape below me. The grass was pleasantly dry – it had been a rainless March and April would be still more arid. Through the gates of Bellahouston Park lorries brought materials and men while the sound of hammering and the noise of drilling came to us on the mild Spring air. "Us" was my Aunt Julia and myself and as she was a school-teacher and it was a weekday, we must both have been on holiday.

Almost as we watched, buildings seemed to advance in preparation. Scaffolders climbed all over the scenic railway, erecting fearsome painted cliffs on its sides and, occasionally, loudspeaker announcements blared. A Post Office telegram delivery boy roared up on a motor-bike importantly and workmen deferentially fell from his path. There was an impression of scurrying, of working against the clock. "Got to be ready for the King and Queen in six weeks," said my aunt.

Going home to Mount Florida that night I was in a fever of impatience for the opening. In the circle of our friends my brothers and I had felt out of things just a little. Many of them already had, or would shortly acquire, season tickets but we would not. My father had just recently bought a pub in Kinning Park (the seller promptly opened a new one at Paisley Road Toll which he christened the Exhibition Bar) and he would be working long and late. There was no possibility that he would be able to escort us. Nor could my mother fill this office as the arrival of her fourth child and our first sister was reasonably imminent. It became clear therefore that our first visit would certainly be under the sheltering wing of the school and it became even clearer to my horror-stricken brothers that they would miss out on grounds of age. Frank, the second boy, was only six and Philip but four, so as I pointed out with sickening logicality, he could hardly expect to go with the school if he wasn't yet at school.

I promised to make a full and accurate report to the under-age members of the family, for up to a point I was sorry for them. I too knew what it was to miss out on occasions of public rejoicing on the simple grounds of being too young. Only the previous year as their Majesties King George VI and Queen Elizabeth were crowned, I had stood in the street watching the tramcars sway past on their way to Rouken Glen and Pollok Estate bearing the triumphal "big boys" who did not forget to wave gloatingly at us small fry. So it was achievement indeed to know that one would be conveyed to the Exhibition.

In the method of conveyance lay the first disappointment of the day. We had confidently expected to be taken to Bellahouston Park on one of the new streamlined Coronation tramcars, the last word in that particular mode of transportation, elegantly slim in appearance, chastely panelled within. As we stood in our straggling lines to be loaded, great was our disgust to see that although the destination board said 'Special' we had been allotted a perfectly ordinary yellow car. Trams were always called cars in Glasgow since very few of the citizens travelled in those other vehicles which have now usurped the name. The different lines were distinguished by colour. As I say, we had a perfectly ordinary yellow car of the kind that had been ferrying citizens to such prosiac destinations as Riddrie and Clarkston since the 1920s. The Corporation was not about to squander the jewels of its Transport Department on a school outing.

The teachers silenced our complaints wearily, they were sufficiently experienced to know that this would be an exhausting day. We ranked no higher in the social scale than Primary Four and were therefore made to travel downstairs. I noticed sullenly that the imposing winter door which separated driver from passengers had been replaced by the little slatted gate that depicted the arrival of summer, although no warm breeze blew along the lower deck but rather the occasional spots of an ambitious drizzle.

Our route baffles me slightly as I look back. Normally one could not go directly to Bellahouston Park from Mount Florida by tramcar but I rather think we did a complicated points-change at Eglinton Toll and then trundled through Pollokshields, wondering at the size of the houses and assuring ourselves that at

The Countess of Elgin cuts the first sod at Bellahouston Park for the start of work on the Empire Exhibition.

THE EMPIRE EXHIBITION OF 1938

least 20 people must live in each one of them. Then the tram turned on to the private track at Mosspark Boulevard – all that meant was that on this short stretch the tramlines ran parallel to the road rather than in the centre of it – and we saw the buildings, which had become familiar to us through newspaper pictures, looming out of the dull summer mist, almost every one topped by an unstirring flag.

We alighted and were counted. Our teachers did their best to ascertain how much money each of us had. In an effort to forestall unseemly competition, two shillings had been laid down as the absolute maximum that any pupil should bring. I was sixpence short of that but there were those who had more than twice the recommended amount. Our immediate demand to be taken to the Amusement Park was met with a quiet but totally firm refusal. In so far as we were reasoned with at all, it was pointed out that the Corporation in its goodness was subsidising (they must have used another word) a considerable part of our admission charges and that this was done to widen our horizons, not so that we could fritter our two shillings away on whirling and sick-making roundabouts. Later in life as a teacher myself I came to realise that those at Bellahouston in charge of us on that day had no wish either to mop up after us or to lose face by turning green themselves if safety dictated that they accompany the more venturesome among us.

We therefore did the "life is real, life is earnest" tour first. We were the formal products of a formal system of schooling and although my school, Holy Cross Primary, was a better social mix than would later be achieved – and certainly an easier one – the boys at least did not dress very differently whether they were the Crosshill sons of doctors and lawyers, the Mount Florida son of a publican or the Govanhill sons of skilled tradesmen and manual labourers. The woollen jersey and matching tie was the almost universal rig of the day and the only major discernible difference was that Crosshill and Mount Florida were shod where Govanhill was booted. Those of us who wore shoes in no way felt superior, quite the reverse. Boots were more satisfactory for playing football, while the tackets on the soles of them could in the hands – more properly feet – of a skilled practitioner, strike a gratifying display of sparks from the neighbourhood pavements. The girls, then as now, were rather more individualistic.

The teachers had a plan of campaign mapped out – it was, looking back, likely that they would have to account closely for their activities on a day which otherwise would have been seen by some of the meaner-minded of their employers as

The Tower of Empire in the building, December 1937.

a skylark. We started with the model of the Victoria Falls which, as we had never seen the real thing impressed us greatly, although we had to pay an entrance fee, not much, but a couple of coppers had gone from the funds. Then in a prearranged order we "did" the Dominions Pavilions.

The Mounties were of interest of course but somehow seemed shorter than those we had seen in films and although a small queue gathered for their autographs I was not of their number. The kangaroo which had been at the Australian Pavilion, tartan-bowed, for the visit of the King and Queen on opening day was not on duty, and in any event said one of the class's season-ticket holders sniffily, his father had told him on their last visit that it was a wallaby.

We liked the Post Office Pavilion with the model aircraft flying about, but we couldn't persuade our teachers to let us queue up for the cinema, although the films on show seemed to be serious enough. Schools and cinemas rarely met in those days, though we were allowed to go once a year in aid of a fund to send poor children to the seaside, the Fresh Air Fortnight it was called, as I remember it. Even then, the film chosen was some grim, remorseless, historical saga such as *Tudor Rose* which concentrated on the unhappy reign of Lady Jane Grey.

We saw Gurkha soldiers and African visitors, although the giraffe-necked women were not ours until late afternoon. As young Glaswegians we were not unused to the sight of Africans and particularly Asians in our streets. The Glasgow docks buzzed with activity and a favourite Sunday walk was to cross the Clyde by the Finnieston ferry then walk down the docks on the other side until finally recrossing the river by the Whiteinch ferry, a fair bit downstream. My father was friendly with a chief steward on the Anchor line and we often got on board ships where the stewards were Indian, Goanese I suppose, and made a great fuss of us three boys which we took exactly as our due and received with a gracious unconsciousness.

In this we were exactly like the other children of our time. Every book we read, every film we saw which had to do with the Empire strengthened our belief that the function of the non-whites in the Empire was to support us to the top of their bent. Good "natives" served us loyally, bad ones plotted against the King-Emperor though sometimes redeeming themselves later on by betraying the plans of their still more evil confederates. The Asian seamen we met on the Glasgow streets, shuffling through the winter weather in freezing, bewildered, miserable groups,

were simply "the coolies". There was nothing whatever consciously demeaning or pejorative in our use of this word for them, we just knew no other.

Scotland was particularly linked to the native peoples of the Empire through missionary work and while the most famous Scottish missionary, David Livingstone, was properly claimed for her own by the Church of Scotland, Catholic schools were far from inactive in the field of conversion. For the last four years I and many of my fellows had been contributing a penny a week towards the Black Babies. Half a crown, or 30 pence old style, baptised a black baby and allowed you to choose his baptismal name. The result was that Kenya, Uganda and parts north were overflowing with Patrick N'Gomos, Ninian Umbulis and Mary Margaret Ndeles. They would live lives of penury under the Empire (as indeed they would have lived them outwith it) but thanks to our pennies they might do better the second time around. Occasionally our missionary zeal faltered and the weekly babies were jelly rather than black but as my aunt taught in my school and had the chance to examine the books, it was vital not to overplay one's hand.

Pavilion succeeded pavilion as we grew hungrier and more eager for the Amusement Park. The inevitable malcontent selected the most obviously posh restaurant – we could imperfectly see elaborately-set tables, with more knives and forks than we knew existed – and wanted to know why we could not eat there. One of our young teachers, Miss Fearon, clearly a headmistress in the making, informed him sweetly that there was no reason whatsoever – if four of us cared to pool our official allowances, one of us could eat. He troubled her no further.

Eventually we ate in a building that seemed to be half-shed, half-marquee. We had our own sandwiches or the great bulk of us did, but the Corporation, commendably realising that there would have been some mouths which might well have gone hungry, had provided a small bag of teabread for each pupil. Ungrateful whelps that we were, we compared this windfall unfavourably to the First Communion breakfasts which had been laid on by the school a few months before. For a start there were no chocolate teacakes, something which no good meal could possibly lack, and in their place were plain cookies which were not easily digestible. Paris buns were better, especially as some of us were perfecting the knack of swallowing them in a "oner". Worst of all, though, the milk which we were to drink with these dainties was off. Nor was it slightly off, no rare thing in those pre-war days in humid, thundery weather. The little third-of-a-pint bottles

PLAN OF EXHIBITION
Selection from the Reference Numbers

- 9 An Clachan (Highland Village)
- 16 Daily Express
- 20 Scottish Pavilion (South)
- 21 Scottish Pavilion (North)
- 24 "The Times"
- 26 Concert Hall
- 27 United Kingdom Government Pavilion
- 32 City of Glasgow Pavilion
- 38 Palace of Industries (West)
- 41 Northern Ireland
- 43 Cinema
- 45 Wool Pavilion
- 46 West African Colonies
- 47 Southern Rhodesia, Victoria Falls and East Africa
- 49 Malaya, British West Indies, Composite Colonial Exhibits
- 50 McCorquodale & Co
- 52 Union of South Africa
- 53 New Zealand
- 54 Canada
- 55 Ireland
- 56 Australia
- 59 Outram Press (Glasgow Herald)
- 61 Imperial Chemical Industries
- 63 Shell-Mex Pavilion
- 64 Beardmore & Colville Pavilion
- 65 Dunlop Pavilion
- 66 Templeton's Pavilion
- 67 Palace of Industries (North)
- 69 Sterne & Co
- 70 Burma
- 79 Grand Staircase
- 81 The Distillers Company
- 82 Chance Brothers
- 88 Palace of Engineering
- 90 Daily Record
- 91 Scottish Motor Traction Company
- 93 The Scotsman
- 94 Coal Pavilion
- 95 Glenfield and Kennedy
- 96 Rubber Pavilion
- 97 Amusement Park
- 99 Dance Hall

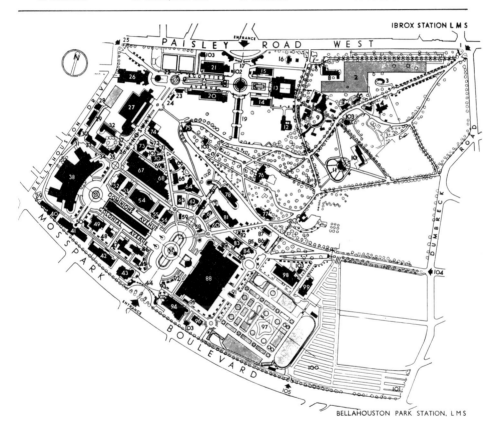

THE EMPIRE EXHIBITION OF 1938

contained something which had approximately the consistency of cheese and seemed to us to have been rejected by another visiting school three weeks before. We said Grace After Meals with a noticeable lack of enthusiasm: unbuttered plain cookies and stiff milk didn't seem worth thanking the Deity for, in our book.

We made a brief, obligatory visit to the Catholic Pavilion. Elsewhere we saw how newspapers were produced and plodded on through the thickening rain, hair falling damply on the brow, dark patches forming on the shoulders of such of us as had trench-coats – the word raincoat was not in usage. A couple of the younger, more fashion-conscious teachers produced a primitive form of pixie-hood to save their perms. The troops began to break ranks and to solicit cigarette-cards from passing men, always a sign that the boredom threshold had been reached. The subjects of the cigarette-cards themselves were changing ominously. Whereas a year or so before we had collected Test cricketers, international footballers and Stars of Stage, Screen and Radio, we now earnestly sought to complete the sets on Air Raid Precautions and Badges of the Royal Air Force. There were still sets which had to do with things peaceful of course and the famous Glasgow tobacco firm, Mitchell's, had brought out its own series of cards which dealt with the buildings of the Empire Exhibition.

The teachers read the signs aright and took us off to see the giraffe-necked women and the attractions of the fairground. We knew a great deal about foreigners from our book, *Life in Many Lands*. We knew that Chinese coolies could carry enormously heavy loads but were unfortunately given to quarrelling and these rammies ended only when one was adjudged to have "lost face", whereupon he ran away in confusion. We would have called it "being shown up" but the concept was familiar to us. Black people in the south of the United States were happy-go-lucky, so said *Life in Many Lands*. All week they chopped cotton quite cheerfully, but at weekends indulged themselves in camp-meetings and dressed themselves in a most flamboyant manner to attend these.

The giraffe-necked women seemed happy enough to our unenquiring eyes for we were now concentrating on the optimum disposal of our remaining monies. Generosity prompted us to take home an Exhibition mug or tea-towel or pencil or lampshade, realism told us that we could (hardly) afford it. I bought a small box of sweets for my mother, knowing that I was the most likely residual beneficiary of my open-handedness. Our season-ticket holders, who had been there before,

An aerial view of the Exhibition Grounds at Bellahouston Park. The White City Stadium and Ibrox Stadium are in the background.

again gave themselves airs as they loudly compared the attractions of the various joyrides which they had sampled on previous visits. One languidly said that the last time he had been at Bellahouston was the day on which Charles Laughton had visited the Exhibition. We suspected he was lying but were not quite sure and we envied him, for Laughton as Captain Bligh in *Mutiny on the Bounty* was part of our stock-in-trade of mimicry: "I'll have one captain on board my ship, Mr. Christian."

We tholed his, the ticket-holder's, superiority because we knew that it carried with it an inherent disadvantage. Every Saturday morning he was dispatched to Bellahouston with instructions not only to look around the Exhibition but to bring home half a pound of bacon from one of the Irish pavilions. After the novelty of the first few Saturdays had worn off he began to feel that he would rather be participating in one of our interminable games of football. Ever resourceful, we suggested that he simply purchase his bacon locally and then join us but he pointed out gloomily that his mother set great store on the authenticity of the purchase and that this was validated by the special bag in which the bacon was wrapped. Any Mount Florida boy worth his salt would have nicked half-a-dozen bags on his next visit to Bellahouston but he was not gifted with that kind of imagination.

There was nobody there of note on that school visit, although later we learned that we had not missed Anna Neagle by much. A few weeks later I attempted to rectify this omission by jumping ship on the night when I was to be confirmed in Holy Cross Church, having learned that Miss Neagle was, however improbably, going to kick-off at the start of a Glasgow Cup match between Third Lanark and Partick Thistle at Cathkin Park. On reflection, her presence there was not at all improbable since she had spent some of her formative years in Mount Florida. Anyway I jumped off another yellow car on the way to receive the episcopal slap but my aunt, she who had sat with me on the slope in High Mosspark, ran after me, grabbed me and, ignoring my eminently reasonable offer to be confirmed the year after, had me done by brute force.

We saw most of the attractions that day with the school but were allowed to board only the most tepid of them. We derived what solace we could by jeering ill-naturedly at a party of boy children from the North of England who had high-pitched voices and corduroy shorts which came to within an inch of the tops of their long stockings. Our scorn on hearing one of them addressed as Clifford was unbounded and we pursued the unfortunate wretch, chanting after him:

ONE OF THE THIRTEEN MILLION

"Aw, Clifford's daddy,
  Is a finnan haddie."

It is impossible that he could have understood our far from received English but he would certainly have realised that we were not conveying expressions of goodwill. Our teachers most certainly realised this and decided that the time had come for the departing muster. We were counted, squared off and marched off to our waiting tramcar. All that remained was to write the obligatory account of our visit, for in the Scottish educational system of those days there was emphatically no such thing as something for nothing.

I came to realise that I enjoyed my later, private, visits to the Exhibition more, not because they were made without classmates but because they took place at night and the very special magic of the Empire Exhibition lay in its lighting. It was possible during the day to be almost unaware of the Tower but in the evenings it dominated everything. Even more wonderful were the fountains with the constantly changing coloured lights and the creeping neon signs which made visual poetry of the most prosaic advertisements. From compliant uncles and aunts concessions could be coaxed and there was nothing this side of the grave to equal one's first turn behind the wheel of one of the Water Dodgems. Motor Dodgems were joy enough but the boats allowed you to assume a careless, nautical air while twisting through the flotilla of enemy craft intent on ramming you to destruction.

Our favourite cousin, Jack, being five years older than I was, came into the category of fit and proper person to take us to Bellahouston. As elsewhere in life there was a price to pay and the promissory note was attendance at the Scout Pageant held at Ibrox Stadium in connection with the Exhibition. I was small but precocious and from very early childhood had harboured feelings of deep antipathy towards the Scouts but although I found them insufferably hearty they were of course part of the necessary apparatus for running the Empire. The Ibrox show was a pageant of Scottish history and as it started with the Druids and I was a keen reader of history even then, we knew that we were in for a long afternoon. The cast list was literally one of thousands and we waited for hours in the sun (it was one of the very few good Saturdays) before Jack's face appeared momentarily before us in the grand march-past. My younger brothers were there that day and we privately thought that it was only a matter of time until the natives of the Empire tumbled to the fact that the Scouts were daft and that the whole thing was worked by mirrors.

No amount of pleading could get us to the Exhibition football matches at Ibrox Park, though Hampden Park would have presented few difficulties. This was especially hard for us to bear as Mount Florida children with a proprietary interest in internationals and Cup finals. We had to be content, like Lochiel, to read of the competing teams' fate in the newspapers or writhe under the excited accounts of our younger uncles.

Over half a century later what does one remember? The things that a greedy eight-year-old would remember – excellent toffee-apples and soft ice cream, the latter new to our experience. A glimpse of a girl muffled in a cloak being escorted through the crowds. She was going to perform feats of acrobatics on a high pole but, alas! in another part of the forest. Bands in military uniforms, playing what we would later realise was eternal military band music, Gilbert and Sullivan, suites and tone pictures by Ketelby, overtures by Suppé. Barkers at work with screeching amplifiers, little trucks conveying passengers throughout the Exhibition, the threat of war and the removal of that threat, the curious notion that we were looking at what New York must be like and an even stranger, because contradictory, impression that we were in the middle of something which was at once fiercely exciting and comfortably safe. And who needed a season ticket anyway?

CHAPTER TWO
PREVIOUS EXPERIENCE

GLASGOW did not come new in 1938 to the running of large-scale international exhibitions. In the great upsurge of civic confidence which characterised the last years of Victoria and the short reign of Edward VII the city has staged three major exhibitions, those of 1888, 1901 and 1911.

The first of these, held in the city's Kelvingrove Park in 1888, was easily the largest to have been held in the British Isles since the Great Exhibition of 1851 in which Victoria's husband, Albert, the Prince Consort, had evinced so keen and continuing an interest. It had not proved easy to induce the Queen to attend for although she had to some extent emerged from her Widow of Windsor period, that time of self-imposed seclusion which followed the death of Albert, she did not move much about her realm and Scotland for her tended to mean Balmoral and very little besides.

Her visit was brief, taking but a day, and it included a token appearance at a Town Council meeting whose carefully abbreviated proceedings might have been copied on future occasions with advantage. Entering the Exhibition grounds by way of the main gate in Kelvingrove Street she received various loyal addresses and songs of praise and in return told the assembly of the great and good that which they already knew, that the Exhibition was the most important to be held in Britain since that of 1851. The occasion was commemorated in the enormous painting done by Sir John Lavery in which oddly enough the faces of the local dignitaries are perfectly clear while that of the monarch can only be discerned with some difficulty. Perhaps in retribution for this reversal of the natural order of things, the painting was so badly damaged during a wartime air-raid of March 1940

THE EMPIRE EXHIBITION OF 1938

that it has been unfit for exhibition ever since, although it remains in the Glasgow Art Galleries in its less than pristine condition. Fortunately Lavery has also left an impression of The Exhibition in his much smaller but extremely evocative painting of *The Exhibition at Night*.

The 1888 Exhibition had been well described by *The Times* as a display of "the wealth, the productive enterprise and the versatility of the great people who flourish under Her Majesty's reign". That of 1901 was to be a more truly international affair. Given the comparatively short time-span between the two exhibitions it is not surprising that the same names tend to figure and indeed both exhibitions had the same President, Sir Archibald Campbell, who by 1901 had become Lord Blythswood.

Again the venue was Kelvingrove Park and the main features of the Exhibition were housed in a giant Industrial Hall whose exterior owed more to Venetian and Eastern palaces than to any close connection with a 19th-century factory. The opening date was Thursday, 9 May, and the King's daughter, the Duchess of Fife, was selected to perform the ceremony together with her husband, the Duke. The city loyally masked any feeling of disappointment that it may have had that the King had not come north in person and in any event his health at that stage was rather precarious. It was a most colourful scene even although all the ladies present at the opening wore half-mourning in memory of the late Queen who had died in January.

The Royal couple were very dutiful in fulfilling this assignment for they returned the following morning to visit the French stands, the Canadian Pavilion, the various Colonial exhibits and the great attraction of the event – the Russian buildings. The special magazine produced for the duration of the Exhibition, *The Exhibition Illustrated* expressed the rather wistful hope that Glasgow might yet see the King: "There is probably some substratum of truth in the rumour that the King, gratified by the splendid welcome given by Glasgow to his daughter, intends to visit the Exhibition in the autumn. His Majesty called upon the Duke and Duchess of Fife the day after their return to the South and doubtless heard all about it. Glasgow is notorious for producing a bad impression on strangers – thanks partly to our climate – but the Duchess, whose first visit it was, had clearly every reason to carry away a bright and pleasing recollection alike of the city and its citizens."

Interspersed with the staid and occasionally sycophantic reporting of the official opening, the authentic voice of Glasgow is heard, refusing to abdicate the critical

The main entrance. This shows the scene shortly before the official opening of the Exhibition. Note the uncovered top decks of the tramcars.

function even in the midst of considerable achievement. It was very possibly a reporter whose allotted place did not realise his own expectations who dipped his pen in vitriol before composing the following, again in *The Exhibition Illustrated*: "The Exhibition authorities seem to have a perfect genius for bungling their purely social functions. So many people of importance were deliberately omitted from the lists of guests invited to the reception in the Art Galleries on the evening of the opening day that one naturally expected to find the *crème de la crème* of Glasgow society within its jealously guarded walls. Yet, as a matter of fact, many young men were present whose 'best' evidently consisted of a new tweed suit and at least one of these was accompanied by his 'girl' in a mackintosh and sailor hat."

The writer had not totally vented his wrath. He went on: "The recommendation that guests should wear 'court dress or uniform' at the reception was apparently construed by some into a licence to wear fancy dress. So at least we interpreted the appearance in Highland costume of sundry citizens whose kinship to the clans it would be hard to discover."

Nor were all the works of building received with universal satisfaction. The same publication, with a candour refreshing in the official organ of the Exhibition had this to say about the grandstand which had been erected for various football matches and athletic meetings, the holding of which set a precedent which would be followed at Bellahouston nearly 40 years later: "The 'Grand' Stand at the new athletic grounds is commodious and looks as if it may afford some shelter. Its 'grandeur' however is mainly in the name. The style of architecture is the Agricultural Renaissance, much employed in farm steadings for the accommodation of straw."

Notwithstanding such acerbic observations the Exhibition went ahead successfully enough. Perhaps a more valid criticism was that of the hours for which the Machinery in Motion Section was open, namely from ten till one, two till five, and six till seven-thirty p.m. It was pointed out with much justification that this effectively prevented working men, who often did not finish until six p.m., from taking advantage of the educational possibilities of the Exhibition. This was a battleground which again would be fought over at Bellahouston in 1938.

While there were complaints that there were inadequate facilities for entertainment, the authorities had made some effort to provide diversion. Ex-Baillie Michael Simons, Convener of the Music, Entertainments, Refreshments and Sports

PREVIOUS EXPERIENCE

Committees and therefore, one suspects, an inordinately busy man, explained what the hope had originally been: "Our original intention had been to illustrate by representative military bands the music of all nations, but I regret to say that, owing to circumstances over which we had no control, the scheme has fallen through."

These circumstances were for the most part political, although not exclusively so, and they illustrate the point that great Exhibitions do not subsist in a vacuum but are affected by the political questions of their day. Chief of these in 1901 was the Boer War. While this conflict ran, Britain was almost friendless in Europe. The King of Belgium refused to sanction the appearance of the band of the Belgian Guides, fearing that the pro-Boer attitude of his countrymen might evoke some ill-feeling at the Exhibition. Kaiser Wilhelm II likewise refused leave to travel to his leading military bands and although purely military reasons were cited, he had sent a telegram of congratulation to President Kruger after a Boer success early in the War.

The French did not play for more practical reasons — a fee could not be agreed. It had been hoped to bring over the band of La Garde Républicaine but their demand for £900 for one week, with travelling expenses in addition, proved quite beyond the purse of the Exhibition committee. There were still distinguished ensembles at Kelvingrove though. These included that led by John Philip Sousa from the United States, leading British bands and several of the most prominent German non-military bands. There had been some ill-feeling because none of the local bands in Scotland had been considered but they were robustly brushed aside as simply not good enough.

Another musical combination which did not meet with any critical acclaim or indeed even common civility was the Hindu band which, representing India, purveyed Eastern music. *The Exhibition Illustrated* had a few barbs specially reserved for them: "Nothing seems capable of quelling the ardour of the Hindoo 'Band' which in the intervals between performances promenades through the grounds discursing 'music'. The pity and the sarcasm of spectators have hitherto been alike unavailing."

The blatant contempt for the exotic and the unfamiliar, doubly strange in an international exhibition, would surface again in 1938, for the tradition that native peoples were objects of fun or distrust was deep-rooted, some might say ineradicable. More tolerance was shown to visiting Europeans who were, after all, much better bets as potential customers: "The Exhibition is to be honoured at an early date by the visit of a number of German naval architects who are to attend the conference in Glasgow. The Hamburg-America steamship *Deutschland* – the fastest steamer in the world – has been placed at their disposal and it is expected that some 260 ladies and gentlemen will avail themselves of the tour which is being organised."

There was a fair amount of what we would call chauvinism and what the Edwardians would indignantly have claimed was patriotism at the 1901 Exhibition. A gun, "Long Tom", captured from the Boers, was a great attraction. So too was the projected visit of Cecil Rhodes and Dr Jameson, he of the famous Raid, who were then shooting in Perthshire.

The prime purpose of the Exhibition was of course the encouragement of industry and commerce and in one respect the response had been disappointing. The greatest industrial nation on the Continent, Germany, was unrepresented. Mr Paul Rottenburg, Convener of the Foreign Committee, had a ready explanation for this: "When the matter of the Glasgow Exhibition was discussed by some of the German firms the question of cost naturally asserted itself. Further, it was found inadvisable, if not impossible to exhibit year after year, and rather than put forward an inadequate and incomplete exhibit the Germans as a nation decided not to show at all. Thus their absence is not due to any feeling, either political or commercial, but simply to considerations of convenience."

For whatever cause, the Germans were a loss and so too were the Belgians who were absent for a different although more intriguing reason. Mr Paul Rottenburg offered this explanation: "Why is Belgium not represented? Simply on account of the Executive having wisely decided to give neither medals or awards of any kind whatsoever. Such proceedings as the appointment of competent jurors, the time occupied in adjudicating, the cost of medals and last but not least the general dissatisfaction of exhibitors when the awards are announced determined the Executive not to make the Glasgow Exhibition a competitive one. When I interviewed the Head of the Department at Brussels and explained to him the details of our scheme he informed me that it would be impossible to obtain the support of Belgium unless awards were given. Consequently, we have had to do without it."

THE EXHIBITION AT NIGHT. *Though not as bright as 1938 would be, the Welsbach Incandescent Light nevertheless provided a remarkable brilliance for its time.*

THE EMPIRE EXHIBITION OF 1938

The Exhibition was mainly a British-Russian affair since the Russians were by far the most important of the foreign exhibitors. Their presentation occupied several buildings and an area of 41,340 square feet, whereas the area taken by the next largest exhibitor, Canada, was scarcely half that at 24,900 square feet. The only other European country to appear on a major scale was France, whose display required 23,500 square feet of space. Australian states exhibited separately, as might have been expected in a country where Federation was so recent, and only two of them did, Queensland and Western Australia.

That being the scale of things – and the only other European entrants were Denmark and Austria with very small displays – what had seemed to be a body blow to the Exhibition, the late opening of the Russian section, turned out to be its redemption. It was not until 11 June that the Russian exhibits were fully ready and this served to revitalise a flagging interest in the events in Kelvingrove Park. The Russian Pavilion was blessed according to the rites of the Orthodox Church and it would be almost the last time that members of the Russian aristocracy would be seen in strength in Britain, certainly in Scotland. Within four years Russia would have been cast as the villain in the Russo-Japanese War, with British sympathies firmly on the side of our Asian allies.

As the crowds came to admire and wonder at the Patent Self-Closing Armoured Fire Doors, the Portable Electric Drills and the New No. 2 Hammond Typewriter, to gaze in awe at the Bedroom Boudoir Furniture, though few of them had a bedroom far less a boudoir, or, in more carefree mood to slide down the giant Water Chute, they could reflect that Glasgow had led the way once again in her capacity as Second City of the Empire, even if it was a pity that Princess Louise had not been able to persuade her father to come north.

Ten years later, the 1911 Exhibition was a rather endearing, lower-key affair which was once more held in Kelvingrove Park and had the benefit of excellent weather, apart from the opening and closing days. It had the laudable purpose of raising funds which would endow a Chair in Scottish History and Literature at Glasgow University and in this it succeeded admirably. The citizens came forward with great liberality, to the extent that the Guarantee Fund which was set at £40,000 actually realised £143,000, or almost four times that amount.

The Exhibition was designed as a celebration of Scotland and its comparatively modest nature was reflected in the choice of royal personages to open it. Whereas

KELVINGROVE OR VENICE? *The Venetian style gondolas were very popular with visitors to the 1901 Exhibition.*

the Prince of Wales had opened that of 1888 and the Princess Louise, Duchess of Fife, that of 1901, the latest was inaugurated by the Duke and Duchess of Connaught. The main building was the Palace or Pavilion of History, as befitted the purpose of the Exhibition and many Scottish historical treasures were therein displayed, such as the letter of 1297 from William Wallace and Andrew Murray to the mayors and communes of Lubeck and Hamburg. Industry too was represented and there was a Highland Clachan erected under the supervision of the man who would re-create the notion for the Empire Exhibition of 1938. In addition to this *Brigadoon*-like hamlet, there was a skilful evocation of a small Lowland town with crow-step gable houses and the medieval Scottish marketing stalls known as Luckenbooths.

The display in Kelvingrove Park did not only look back. Three years before, Blériot had crossed the Channel by air and there was an Aviation Pavilion. This had on show a monoplane, a bi-plane, a Pilcher glider and a Zeppelin airship.

There was a foreign presence at the Exhibition, though not a particularly strong one. It included, however bizarrely, a party of tribesmen from Senegal in West Africa. In the course of the Exhibition a child was born to the wife of a Lebou warrior and in a delightful newspaper error of the time "christened according to Mohammedan rites". The unlucky child emerged from this "christening" with the totally incongruous name of Waverley Mamadou Diop. Worse still, this hideously inappropriate name had been arrived at as the result of a competition – Waverley triumphed because it formed the initial letters of West African Village Exhibition Real Live Ebony Youngster. The chief of the tribe was given as a memento of this event a copy of *Waverley*, by Sir Walter Scott, in French. It may be doubted whether a less appropriate gift was ever bestowed since the ramifications of Jacobite intrigue can hardly have been a matter of prime concern in West Africa despite the Prince's involvement with the chief's imperial masters.

A Glasgow journalist of the day, Donald Muir, gives an interesting glimpse of the crowds who went to Kelvingrove and of their curiously stratified behaviour: "So the battalions pass through Kelvingrove in their exclusive sets and separate circles, jostling but never intermixing. There is magnificence and arrogance – the easy expenditure of the rich and sometimes a foolish extravagance on the part of the poor. And there is honest poverty which scorns to ape that which it is not

PREVIOUS EXPERIENCE

. . . By ten o'clock the fair ends. The music ceases, the fountains make their last few feeble splashes, the glow-worm lights around the ponds burn out, the battalions swarm into the streets around the waiting cars and are borne away and, for a few hours, repose settles on Kelvingrove."

The last few weeks of the Exhibition of 1911 were an anti-climax. It had opened on 3 May, the very day on which the Empire Exhibition would open 27 years later, but an attempt had been made to keep it running into November and the weather proved the folly of this experiment. On the night the gates closed for the last time there was a violent storm which blew the roofs off the Aviation Pavilion and the Industrial Hall. It also caused a wall of the Palace of History to collapse but fortunately none of the priceless historical exhibits were lost or even damaged.

The whole affair had been rather muted in comparison with the two great preceding shows, yet almost nine-and-a-half million people had attended in the 160 days. From the ranks came the perennial cry of "not enough bread, not enough circuses" but most people seemed to have enjoyed themselves even if the feeling was of a display which was slightly staid, and rather "worthy". In any event, and most importantly, Glasgow University had its Chair of Scottish History and Literature.

The red lion above the entrance gate welcomed visitors to the Exhibition.

CHAPTER THREE
THE IDEA TAKES SHAPE

CHARLES A. Oakley, one of the very few men living in Glasgow in 1988 who took an active part in the Empire Exhibition, is emphatic that the driving force behind it was Sir James Lithgow of the famous shipbuilding family. As the months and years progressed and the international situation worsened during the 1930s. Lithgow was increasingly needed by the Government for work of national importance and so the spokesmen for the Exhibition tended to be its President, Lord Elgin, and Cecil M. Weir, the Convener of the Exhibition Committee. But that the initial conception was that of Sir James Lithgow, Charles Oakley has no doubt whatsoever.

The motivation was commercial and industrial. No area in Britain had suffered more severely from the Great Depression of the 1930s than the West of Scotland, Shipbuilding had contracted, the Lanarkshire mines were in their last throes and major undertakings such as Stewart and Lloyd's, the great iron and steel works, had chosen to re-locate in the south, in this particular instance in Corby in Northamptonshire. Prestige projects such as the building of the giant Cunarder at John Brown's Shipyard in Clydebank – as yet unnamed and known only by her order book number of 534 – had come to a halt on account of the nation's perilous financial position and for months the huge hulk lay unfinished on the stocks. When eventually permission was given to recommence work on her, the running feet of the shipyard workers on the first morning passed into Clydeside legend. So depressed was the shipbuilding trade that another world-famous Clyde shipyard was working on a solitary order and that was a Clyde paddle-steamer.

By 1938 things were improving, although still very slowly. It has to be remembered that almost two years after the close of the Exhibition there would still be a million unemployed in Great Britain in the very month of Dunkirk, May 1940. It was felt that the trade recovery of Scotland was lagging behind that of London and particularly that of the Midlands where the new motor industries were firmly establishing themselves.

The first formal steps towards holding an Exhibition arose from a meeting in Merchants' House, Glasgow, sponsored by the Scottish Development Council. The Earl of Elgin voiced what was in the minds of many people. "The effort must embrace Scotland as a whole, it must aim at expanding Scottish industry and employment and must not overlook the great asset Scotland has in its charm of scenery and opportunities for holiday sport and pleasure."

The first question to be decided was what kind of an Exhibition should be held. An international exhibition was not practicable because under the strict international rules for holding these, there would be no vacancy until 1947. An exhibition which confined itself within the bounds of the Empire would be exempt from such regulation while still being large enough in all conscience. The population of the Empire was currently recorded as 66 million white and 384 million coloured souls and in extent it covered one-quarter of the land surface of the globe.

It was a rare window of opportunity. Cecil M. Weir spoke vehemently in favour of action: "There are few if any other competing attractions planned in other countries for 1938 and coming so early in the reign of the King-Emperor it would be a fine gesture to the world of the peaceful industrial confidence of the United Kingdom and the Empire overseas and of the undiminished courage, enterprise and resource of the Scottish people."

This speech was given on 5 October 1936 and interestingly the King-Emperor referred to was Edward VIII who was to abdicate from that office within two months. The country then underwent the shock of the Abdication but although there was a momentary loss of confidence in commerce, things soon righted themselves. More than that, the Government was not averse to giving its approval to a major event which would enable a little-known new monarch who was paralysingly shy to be seen by his subjects in favourable surroundings. At that time it was still considered possible, however unlikely it seems now, that a King's Party might arise which would wish to bring back the exiled Duke of Windsor. The fact that Queen Elizabeth had been brought up in Scotland and that the younger daughter, Princess Margaret Rose, had been born in her mother's

Not an exhibit that went wrong but the Crazy House in process of construction.

ancestral home at Glamis Castle in Angus, only made the Glasgow project that much more attractive.

That inaugural meeting then passed to the question of financing the projected Exhibition. This topic was approached in a spirit of optimism. All three previous Glasgow exhibitions had shown a profit, that of 1901 had made a surplus of £30,000 on a subscription guarantee of £509,000 and the more modest affair of 1911 had nevertheless been in the black to the extent of £15,000. It was decided that the guarantee fund should be £500,000 and it was started with two donations of £10,000 each from Lord Weir of G. & J. Weir Ltd of Cathcart, the noted manufacturers of pumps, and from Sir Harry McGowan of ICI. It was vitally important that two points be stressed from the outset, first that the Exhibition involved not just Glasgow but the whole of Scotland and second that this was an Exhibition for the whole of the Empire which happened to be taking place in Glasgow. The method of guarantors with a purely nominal capital had been chosen in preference to the formation of a company with a large share issue on the grounds of expense.

The next question to be decided was that of site. The traditional venue, Kelvingrove Park, was now far too built up to be in any way suitable and one or two other parks available to the Committee, such as Rouken Glen, were located at the very edge of the city. It was therefore decided to approach the Corporation of Glasgow for a lease of Bellahouston Park in the south-west of the city. Before doing this the pros and cons of such a move had been canvassed.

Bellahouston could certainly provide the space needed – it would eventually yield 175 acres, much of it on the flat. A fairly high hill afforded both focus and vantage point. It was well-served by Glasgow's public transport system which at that time could fairly claim to be ranked among the best of such systems in any country or continent. Tramcars and buses passed the gates, the park was within walking distance of two of the stations on the city's diminutive subway system and there was the possibility, which later came to pass, that a new railway station could be built at Ibrox on the line between Glasgow and Paisley. Ibrox could prove useful in another connection. It was the home of Rangers Football Club who owned a massive and well-equipped football ground which had not infrequently accommodated six-figure crowds. It would be the ideal venue for the official opening and any large-scale pageants that might be held as part of the Exhibition. King George VI is credited with the suggestion that the opening should be held there but this

THE IDEA TAKES SHAPE

The view from the Grand Staircase looking south towards the entrance. Basil Spence's ICI Pavilion and the Palace of Engineering, attributed to Launcelot Ross, may be seen to the left of the picture.

seems unlikely. There was the possibility, which in the event was not put into effect, of linking the Stadium, as it became known around this time, with Bellahouston Park by means of an overhead bridge.

These were the plusses. As counter-balance the park was fully two miles distant from the city centre and although the immediate surroundings of the area were pleasant, the drive out through Tradeston and Plantation would bring the overseas visitor in the closest of contact with some of the worst housing in the Western world. People would not be able to drop in for a couple of hours as they had done at Kelvingrove. Would enough of them be found who would make a day of it out at Bellahouston? Then again, the park stood in the middle of a residential area, and more than that a "dry" one. There were no licensed premises in the immediate vicinity and the inhabitants of Mosspark and Pollokshields preferred it that way.

Yet an Exhibition which could not sell drinks, or, as the hypocritical Glasgow phrase had it "refreshments", was surely foredoomed to failure. This was a problem that would have to be tackled.

The decision to proceed had been taken. Even £250,000 would be a sufficient sum on which to act, although £500,000 would clearly be better. Should there be a surplus it would be applied by the Scottish Development Council to purposes calculated to benefit the whole country. In a clever tactical ploy the formal proposal to go ahead was moved by Lord Provost Gumley of Edinburgh, emphasising that the undertaking was national rather than local. Lord Provost Stewart of Glasgow contented himself with seconding.

The decision was well-received. A leader article in the *Glasgow Herald* next day commented that "Scotland is not in any sense down and out . . . At the moment she can truthfully be said to be on the upgrade." Things were beginning to happen. The Corporation of Glasgow gave its approval for the use of Bellahouston on 7 October 1936 and, just as gratifying, the guarantors were coming forward in numbers. Before the end of November the desired half-million pounds had been exceeded and the list of subscribers reads like a war memorial to Scottish industry, with large subscriptions from J. and P. Coats of Paisley, the Coltness Iron Company, Fairfield Shipbuilding Company, India of Inchinnan, the tyre firm, the Imperial Tobacco Company and a host of others.

Largest of all private donations was one of £20,000 from the motor industry magnate and philanthrophist, Lord Nuffield, but Edinburgh Town Council showed an admirable willingness to become involved with their own donation of £10,000. Glasgow, more closely concerned, contributed £25,000 and some firms still in existence, prominent among them the Distillers' Company Limited and Babcock and Wilcox, also provided five-figure sums. Indeed £100,000 had already been promised by the time the appeal officially opened on 20 October 1936 with this ringing message: "The Scottish Development Council has come to the opinion that there are no better means of advertising the industries and resources of Scotland than by the holding of the Empire Exhibition which will proclaim the industrial and cultural genius of the Scots people and promote the increase of trade between the United Kingdom and the Empire."

It was time to appoint an architect and a manager. The architect was Thomas Tait, who had a global reputation and had been responsible for the design of

THE IDEA TAKES SHAPE

The Castle of the Glen, the big house which dominated the Clachan.

Sydney Harbour Bridge a few years before. Nearer home he had been commissioned to design St Andrews House in Edinburgh, the great headquarters of the Civil Service in Scotland, on a site opposite Calton Hill. This massive building would be opened by His Royal Highness the Duke of Gloucester in 1939. Tait would make a considerable impression at Bellahouston, particularly with the great Tower which was the centrepiece of the Exhibition, the rather grandiloquently named Tower Of Empire. As manager, the Executive Committee lighted upon Captain S. J. Graham from the Exhibitions Division of the Department of

Overseas Trade. He had been heavily involved with the Wembley Exhibition of 1925 and the New Zealand and South Seas Exhibition at Dunedin the following year.

Meanwhile the position of the Labour councillors within the Corporation of Glasgow was a shade ambivalent. They could hardly be seen openly to oppose a venture which had as its aim the restoration of employment but they not unnaturally distrusted anything which originated from the Chamber of Commerce. Sir James Lithgow too was suspect for having reduced wages in the shipyards during the severe depression of the early 1930s. Patrick Dollan, City Treasurer and later to be Lord Provost, was rather more visionary than most of his colleagues. A journalist by training, he could see the enormous publicity gains to be had from a successful Exhibition although he made it very clear, in a speech on 23 October 1936, that the Corporation had other things to do than actually to run the Exhibition. Nevertheless a Corporation Coordinating Committee was formed which in addition to Patrick Dollan, included three other future Lord Provosts – Jean Roberts, Tom Kerr and Victor D. Warren. They must have been heartened by Captain S. J. Graham's speech the following month in which he stated that the Empire Exhibition would give direct employment to some 5,000 people but they would not have been nearly as responsive to the notion that Trade Unions should allow some measure of dilution for the construction workers who would be required to get the Exhibition ready in time for the opening in May 1938.

By the time 1937 arrived more than £600,000 had been raised in guarantees and both sides were getting down to discuss details. It was estimated that the cost of erecting the Exhibition buildings, of which two – the Palace of Arts and the Tower – would be permanent structures would be in the region of £350,000 to £400,000. The promoters of the Exhibition would bear the costs of any repairs or replacements and any expense involved in the reasonable and practical restoration of the ground to its original use as a public park. Surprisingly, in an age when ownership of motor cars was severely restricted, there was to be parking space provided for 10,000 vehicles.

The projected attendance was set at 20 million and appeals were made to householders to place accommodation at the disposal of those who might be coming from overseas. Golf clubs were urged by the Scottish Golf Union to offer the courtesy of their courses to overseas visitors, a request which was forcefully and sometimes

The "daemonic verticality" of Tait's Tower is in severe contrast to the traditional building of the Clachan.

THE EMPIRE EXHIBITION OF 1938

counter-productively backed up by the Corporation of Glasgow. For those at the top end of the market, a brand new hotel had been built in Glasgow in much the same architectural style that was to dominate the Exhibition. The Beresford Hotel in Sauchiehall Street had 324 rooms and a telephone in each and every one of them.

In the spring of 1937 the Countess of Elgin ceremonially turned the first sod on the site at Bellahouston and from then on events moved swiftly. A great hurdle was cleared when three months before the Corporation decided not to oppose the granting of liquor licences. This was not a decision which was endorsed unanimously, Councillor James Gray of Cathcart thundering, "I believe that the presence of public houses in the Empire Exhibition would be a menace not only to the Exhibition but also to the community." There were similar predictable and fruitless protests from the Scottish Temperance Alliance and the Pollokshields Ward No-Licence Committee. In the event these misgivings proved ill-founded for out of the first 300,000 visitors who attended the Exhibition there were only three arrests for drunkenness and one of these offenders offered the excuse that "he had been overcome with joy at the sight of the Exhibition." He deserved to be exonerated if only for effrontery.

Even this modest number of inebriates was to prove too much for 'Glengarry' who in a letter to the *Evening Times* of 10 May fumed: "Here is evidence that for the first three days of the Exhibition three drunks came before the criminal court. That means there will be 156 drunks in court over the six months of the Exhibition. Such a record would not be a credit but a black spot in the history of the Exhibition which a financial success could never blot out."

The Corporation was anxious that the city should benefit after the Exhibition had moved on and that, if possible, it should inherit some facilities. The suggested provision of a permanent swimming pool, a "Glasgow Lido", was knocked back, nor was the Corporation Exhibition Sub-Committee any more fortunate with its plea for the establishment of a nursery school and child welfare centre. It is ironic that the only permanent legacy of the Exhibition which the city inherited, the Palace of Arts, has never been used for the purpose for which it was built, as an overflow to accommodate and display the surplus pictures held at the Glasgow Art Galleries in Kelvingrove.

It would be maintained with some bitterness that the London newspapers, magazines and radio ignored the events at Bellahouston in 1938 and that this

THE IDEA TAKES SHAPE

neglect was deliberate and founded on a fear that the Exhibition would compare too favourably with that at Wembley in 1925 which had been far from an unqualified success. Stanley Baldwin, then Prime Minister, did his best to help when at the Empire Day banquet on 24 May 1937 he told the Dominion Prime Ministers who had come over for the coronation of King George VI: "Warm as your welcome has been in London, you will be astonished by the welcome you will get from the Scots. They'll love to see you. They have asked me to give you this message."

Gradually, construction details began to be fed to a fascinated public. The Palace of Engineering would have a frontage of 465 feet, would occupy five acres and the laying of foundations would entail the excavation of 8,000 tons of earth. In June work would start on the building of the Tower, soon to be the focus of all eyes and a constant Glasgow talking-point. Its construction would enable Scottish steel companies to show their enduring skills. It would be almost 300 feet high, would have three balconies near the top to which visitors would be conveyed by electric lifts and the walls of its restaurants would be of glass. This was how the more prosperous future was going to look in Scotland.

The main approach road from the city centre, Paisley Road West, was to be widened for a mile to the west of Lorne Street. There was little that could be done about the houses lining the route but at least distinguished visitors might now pass them more quickly. For those workers huddled into the tenements of Plantation and Kinning Park, there would be a reminder in the Clachan of the kind of housing from which many of their forebears had escaped.

The Clachan was a repeat of the successful "dream village" which had formed part of the Kelvingrove Park Exhibition of 1911. It purported to show a cross-section of Highland housing and its nine buildings ranged from the traditional "black house" with earth floor, dear to every Scot who was not called upon to inhabit one, to a "big house", a pre-Reformation "cill" or church, a smithy and a modern cottage. This look-back on times past would be all the more effective for being within shouting distance of the modern industrial estate at Hillington which the Scottish Industrial Estates Company had recently established and which was so extensive that it had three-and-a-half miles of roads.

Inevitably the Clachan roused passions and raised temperatures. For many it was the absolute antithesis of the Scotland the Exhibition was trying to promote. Yet although Gaels and Lowlanders argued furiously over the authenticity or even desirability of its features, it is probable that the stream, the hump-backed bridge, the ceilidhs in the chief's castle and the black houses would be remembered by many visitors long after they had forgotten the contents of the pavilions. It was an exhibition village, true, but never solely or merely a museum piece.

As 1938 began, various panics set in. An exhibition must open to time and be fully ready for business. This did not happen very often. Men thought back to the delayed opening of the Russian section at Kelvingrove in 1901. They did not need to go anything like as far back. Wembley had opened in a state of unpreparedness, while in France in 1937 the joke had been that it was known as the Paris Expo . . . because it was never finished.

Gallingly, for an event which was to be plagued by weather which was persistently abominable, the Spring of 1938 was uniformly sunny and warm. There was a *frisson* of alarm when Hitler marched into Austria in March but things re-established themselves for all except the Jewish community. April was the sunniest ever known and the sun poured down to such an extent that a few days before the off the specially raised plants were wilting in the heat. The plants may have wilted but the buildings shot up, delayed only by the ritualistic strikes designed to force overtime payments from the contractors. There was plenty of overtime, and Sunday working too, which seems to have passed almost unnoticed.

The minds of men were now firmly fixed on the opening. No Exhibition in Scotland had ever been opened by a reigning monarch before and as if to make up for that omission the whole Royal Family – King, Queen and two princesses – were to make the trip north to Glasgow, though in the event the Royal children were left behind. It would be such a day of pageantry as Glasgow had seldom seen, and to enable people to benefit to the utmost from it there was the suggestion that 3 May should be declared a public holiday for those in work and even for those not so fortunate. The apparent contradiction is solved in this declaration from R. D. Crook, the General Secretary of the Ministry of Labour Association: "I urge that the opening day of the Empire Exhibition should be a public holiday. Labour Exchanges should be shut, the unemployed should not be required to sign the unemployed register that day. They should be free to take whatever part they can with their limited resources in the Empire Exhibition and its celebrations."

THE IDEA TAKES SHAPE

Aerial view of the Exhibition looking north. The bi-plane did not have too much time remaining to it.

At the other end of the social scale, questions of dress were exercising both the *Evening Times* and the Duke of Montrose. The newspaper took a sarcastic and unworthy swipe at Labour councillors by wondering whether on the great day they would wear "a lum hat, a soft hat or just a bunnet"? All of these would have been wrong in the opinion of His Grace of Montrose. He announced that Highland dress would be the correct thing for gentlemen entitled to wear it and stated that His Majesty had graciously approved this. Then as now Royalty gave gracious approval rather than unqualified assent. The Duke gave his reasons: "I myself will wear the kilt and I hope others will follow this example for which the King has graciously given approval so that it may convey a living impression to our many visitors of Lord Elgin's happy phrase 'Scotland at home to the Empire'."

In anticipation and a certain amount of trepidation, Scotland gave the house a final dusting-over, dressed herself in her variegated best and sat expectant. The next knock at the door would be a royal one.

City centre pavement. The crowd watching the Royal procession leave Central Station. The soldiers are still putteed.

CHAPTER FOUR
OVERTURE AND BEGINNERS

THE formal opening of the Empire Exhibition was due to take place on 3 May 1938 and the main worry of the promoters was the continuation of the unprecedently dry weather. April had been of a surpassing brilliance with 163.2 hours of sunshine as against 66.2 the previous year. Other statistics were even more impressive – 23 dry days as against 14 and 0.68 inches of rain against 1.92. As one small illustration of how unseasonable the weather had been, the blacksmith in the Clachan had been unable to make trial of his forge because of the danger to the thatched roofs from fire.

On the morning of the opening the King and Queen drove through the streets of Glasgow in the Ascot landau from the city centre out to Ibrox Stadium. There they were received by the customary guard of honour and a rapturous welcome from the crowd. Sir Harry Lauder had been almost as warmly received when he demonstrated a few Highland dance steps on the way to his seat. The Royal couple had arrived at Central Station at ten o'clock and were in the stadium 35 minutes later. There they were officially welcomed by the Earl of Elgin and Kincardine, the President of the Exhibition. A 21-gun salute was fired and all flags were broken out as a fanfare sounded. Psalm 24 was sung to the tune of St George's, Edinburgh, the Moderator of the General Assembly of the Church of Scotland offered a prayer and it was time for the King's speech.

This was a matter of some anxiety for it was known that King George VI, who is his youth had suffered from a marked speech impediment, found public speaking something of a trial. In his uniform of Admiral of the Fleet, he now rose formally to inaugurate the Exhibition. He spoke briefly and well; in the *Movietone Newsreel*

THE EMPIRE EXHIBITION OF 1938

of the event, only the tight gripping of his sword-handle betrays any sense of strain. The main thrust of his speech is contained in this extract: "It is a significant fact that the plans were being prepared at a time when this country was still under the cloud of a long industrial depression. For this reason alone, many people would have hesitated to embark on a scheme of so wide and formidable a scope. But, in addition, the fact had to be faced that the Exhibition would inevitably challenge comparison with those held at Wembley, in New Zealand and in South Africa... Scotland was not daunted, for that has never been her way. She believes that the best means of avoiding trouble is to provide against it and that new enterprise is the safest insurance against the return of depression... Just as men and women have gone out from Scotland in the past to found a new home in countries overseas so I hope that this Exhibition, built by their descendants, will attract to Scotland many visitors from those distant lands. To those who come from foreign countries I can promise a cordial welcome. I am sure they will not be disappointed in what they find."

The Royal Party then departed for the short drive to Bellahouston Park, their coach pursued by running youngsters who would perhaps never expect to see the monarchs again in those pre-television days. At the Exhibition grounds the King and Queen made several joint visits before pursuing separate itineraries. Both inspected the Clachan where a noted Gaelic singer from Barra, Mary Morrison, sang the *Farewell to Barra*, much to the Queen's approval. Perhaps with some judicious prompting, perhaps not, for King George VI shared his family's gift of recall for names, he was introduced to a radio operator he "remembered" who had been aboard HMS *Collingwood* at the Battle of Jutland in which ship the King had also been under fire. Their Majesties were greeted at the St Kilda Cottage by Finlay McQueen, "King" of St Kilda until its evacuation only some seven years before. In the Gaelic which was his only tongue he murmured, "God bless you both and your family."

The Royal visit had got the Exhibition off to the best of starts. The Queen was at her best on such occasions and the newspapers had played up the Scottish links for all they were worth. She endeared herself to her subjects by patting a kangaroo at the Australian Pavilion – the animal Aussie, bedecked for the occasion in a tartan bow, was also rewarded by the Queen with raisins – and the King made himself even more popular with Exhibition officials by writing in the Visitors'

OVERTURE AND BEGINNERS

Good morning, Your Majesties. These Cub Scouts will not be faulted for want of enthusiasm.

Book: "Much better than Paris or Wembley." Nor was this necessarily simply good-mannered flattery on the part of a guest, at least Bellahouston had opened on time and ready for action. Great offence was caused when two prominent London newspapers could only highlight that some of the wilting plants had had to be removed to the back of buildings out of the royal line of sight.

The King and Queen had lunched within the Exhibition grounds at the striking Atlantic Restaurant, which, designed like the bow of a ship, projected from the base of a little hill to the west of the Tower of Empire. The nautical illusion was heightened by the fact that the catering staff were not only dressed as stewards and stewardesses but actually were such, employees of the Anchor Line which plied between Glasgow, North America and India. The royal couple had dined from a menu which only lightly looked towards Scotland. Beginning with caviar, they had then moved on to Tay salmon, lamb, peas, potatoes, asparagus, soufflé and coffee.

At 3.45 p.m. the Royal Party left from the newly built railway halt at Ibrox to visit the new industrial estate of Hillington before continuing to Paisley Unemployed Mens' Club. It was to be the first of many Royal visits to the Exhibition and nothing would be more strange than the great affinity which in particular Queen Mary was to develop towards it. These visits were made easier for the officials by the fact that security in 1938 was minimal. Pictures and newsreels of the time consistently show a couple of distinctly overweight policemen lumbering into view, usually after the Royal car has passed.

Various foreign monarchs and princes were reported to be coming, among them King Carol and Prince Michael of Rumania, King Boris of Bulgaria and King Leopold and Prince Charles of Belgium. In the event none did and within 12 years none of the three monarchs was in possession of his throne.

The organisers could now heave a sigh of relief for Royal visits, though enjoyable, are by their nature fraught. Early indications were good, good as the weather to that stage. By mid-April 120,000 season tickets had been sold, 97,000 of them on the instalment system. What was the visitor to Bellahouston able to see?

If he entered from the Paisley Road side he was likely to notice first the Palace of Arts, one of the two permanent structures in the grounds. One of the aims of the Exhibition was to instruct painlessly, for as a *Glasgow Herald* leader article of the time said, "It is doubtful if the pill of knowledge has ever before been so attractively presented." The same paper in its Exhibition Supplement went on to chide: "There are really very few people who know what they should about the giants of Scottish painting . . . it is just this sort of vagueness that the historical section of the Palace of Arts is designed to correct."

There was certainly an impressive concentration of known painters and paintings. Ramsay, Raeburn, Wilkie, McTaggart senior, the Glasgow School – with Lavery and Sir James Cuthrie the most prominent – and coming nearer 1938 Hornel and E. A. Walton. Other artists on show were J. G. Pringle, S. J. Peploe, Leslie Hunter and Duncan Grant of the notorious Bloomsbury Set. The *Herald*

Limbless and wounded ex-Servicemen of World War 1 at the official opening at Ibrox Park of the Empire Exhibition.

article concluded its rather hectoring information-giving by a proud claim: "The Palace of Arts is one of the permanent buildings of the Empire Exhibition. Unfortunately it will not eventually include the collection of art treasures it holds for the next six months. It will serve as a badly needed overflow for Kelvingrove Art Galleries *(itself the product of the Exhibition of 1901)* and that is a good enough start for any Palace of Arts and a better start than Kelvingrove itself had. And we will stand by our claim that it is now the best provincial art gallery in the country."

Not everyone was of the same opinion regarding the calibre of paintings selected for display within the Palace of Arts. Even among Scots there was no unanimity.

THE EMPIRE EXHIBITION OF 1938

George Scott-Moncrieff, writing in the *Scottish Field* was perhaps the most trenchant dissenter: "Here was a great opportunity for discrimination and escape from Municipal-Gallerydom and instead the walls have been hung thick with a wearisome and doitering collection which is at least ten times as big as it should be." This advocate of the strange and new then happily went on to contradict himself within the next few sentences: "Quite the best exterior is that of the South African Pavilion which is of course strictly traditional in its design."

By now, the visitor, bemused, might well have passed on from this, as Mr Scott-Moncrieff would have had it, over-indulgence in paintings. What lay ahead for him or her?

The Pavilions fell into three categories, those of the Dominions and individual Colonies, those devoted to sectors of human activity such as Industry, Arts and Engineering and those mounted by individual firms in commerce and communications. As might have been expected there were two Scottish Pavilions, which contained not only modern exhibits but rare books and a Hall of Heraldry. A prominent Glasgow department store, Copland and Lye, had engaged Willie Meikle, the most famous of the Kilbarchan hand-loom weavers, to weave tartan on a loom which was more than two centuries old.

On Dominion Avenue the major countries of Empire had their sites. The Canadian Pavilion had a tower 100-feet high and over the main entrance a ten-foot golden symbol of Canadian youth. The materials and furnishings were exclusively Canadian and the great draw of this particular pavilion for young visitors was the presence at all times of two Canadian Mounted Policemen on duty. So popular did the Mounties, drawn from the Saskatoon depot, become that they had to be specifically prohibited from signing autographs for their young admirers, otherwise they would have been completely prevented from carrying out their duties.

The Australian Pavilion included a large-scale model of the recently opened Sydney Harbour Bridge, of all the more interest to the visitors to the Exhibition because the same architect, Thomas S. Tait had been engaged on both projects. Background music was fittingly provided by records of Australian artists such as Dame Nelly Melba, Florence Austral and Peter Dawson. As well as the kangaroo which had taken the Queen's fancy on opening day, the pavilion also included opals to the value of £20,000. It was perhaps the reputation of these stones as

OVERTURE AND BEGINNERS

The KING SPEAKS. *H.M. King George VI, speaking at Ibrox Park, formally declares open the Empire Exhibition of 1938.*

bringers of ill-fortune that protected them against the depredations of the pickpockets and sneak thieves, "four in number and all from London", as the *Evening Times* noted smugly. They were sentenced to hard labour for their activities at the Exhibition. It is worth mentioning that to reassure the timorous the Exhibition had been given its own police presence and fire brigade, but in fact the crowds were wonderfully well-behaved and the great majority of arrests were for illegal taking of bets, the "bookie's runner" being very much then part of the Glasgow street scene.

The New Zealand Pavilion was fronted by two pillars of Maori design and its most notable exhibit was a model of the longest railway tunnel within the Empire. The Burma Pavilion was sufficiently pagoda-like to be of intriguingly exotic interest and it had a special attraction for Scots in that the headquarters of the Burmah Oil Company were in Glasgow and the proportion of Scots among the expatriates there had always been high.

With a traditional lack of logic, the Irish Free State, known now as Eire, had a large pavilion at the Exhibition although in many aspects it was not a member of the Empire. It is true that ties would not formally be severed until 1949 when Eire became the Republic of Ireland, but the Governor-General had already gone, as had the King's head from stamps and the coinage. In the course of the Exhibition

THE EMPIRE EXHIBITION OF 1938

year British troops, the last in the Free State, were leaving those very ports which the Irish Government would refuse to make available to Britain when war came less than a year later. More important perhaps than these external signs was Article 2 of the Dublin Government's new constitution of 1937 which stated quite unambiguously: "The national territory consists of the whole island of Ireland, its islands and the territorial seas." Given all this and the fact that there were very few inhabitants of the 26 Counties who would have described themselves in 1938 as subjects of the British Empire the Irish presence could only be regarded as unexpected.

The two countries were just emerging from a damaging trade war and the traditional agricultural products of Ireland did well. There was an indication that Eire would not always be a backward, predominantly agricultural state, for pride of place among the exhibits went to a model of the massive Shannon Power Scheme which had been begun by German engineers in 1925 and brought to a successful conclusion.

There was also a Northern Ireland Pavilion which exhibited not only agricultural products but those of the traditional Ulster industries, linen, tobacco and shipbuilding, in addition to the newer but very important revenue-earner, tourism. An agreeable feature of the Exhibition was that the Lord Mayors of Dublin and Belfast paid a joint visit and toured both pavilions extremely amicably.

By far the most striking of the Dominion Pavilions was the South African one, built in the style of a traditional Cape Dutch farmhouse and of great distinction. It held a replica of the Koh-i-Noor and the building itself is one of the few to have survived to this day, though in drastically altered form. For many years it was used as a guest-house by ICI at their premises in Ayrshire.

The observant reader will have noticed that there has been no mention of what should perhaps have been the largest pavilion of all, that of India. The reason for this is very simple: India absolutely declined to take part in the Exhibition, a signal perhaps that there were not many days left to the Raj on the sub-continent.

The Rhodesian Pavilion had as its great attraction a model of the Victoria Falls, an interesting piece of private enterprise on the part of two young South Africans, Mormal (sic) Yule and Roderick Sechel and for which a separate charge for admission was made, to widely-voiced discontent. Most Scots must have fought down their traditional canniness, however, for the show was an enormous financial success, grossing £1,600 per week.

The Queen with the Countess of Elgin and Sir James Lithgow at the Empire Exhibition, Glasgow – 1938.

THE EMPIRE EXHIBITION OF 1938

The smaller colonies of course could not sustain separate pavilions and tended to be grouped together. Southern Rhodesia and East Africa made some sense but there was a hint of desperation and catch-all in the Colonial Pavilion which yoked Malta, Somaliland, Hong Kong and the Falkland Islands in quadruple harness.

The Women of the Empire Pavilion, of which the Queen was the special patron, ran displays by the Women's League of Health and Beauty, led by Prunella Stack who would shortly marry Lord David Douglas-Hamilton, fourth son of the Duke of Hamilton. With a nice sense of historical continuity an exhibition of costume included the crinoline which Queen Victoria had worn to the opening of the Great Exhibition of 1851.

The Empire Tea Pavilion was extremely popular, not only because it dispensed free samples but because in the early days of the Exhibition it was one of the few places where a meal could be had for what was regarded as a reasonable price. Under the auspices of the Samuel Johnson Society, for the great lexicographer and philosopher had been a noted tea-drinker, a competition was held to find the world's largest teapot. The official claimant was a teapot which held three-and-a-half gallons and could provide one hundred cups of tea at a filling. Other contenders came from all over Britain, including one from the headline-hunting highly eccentric Glasgow businessman and A. E. Pickard. There were valuable hand-painted Staffordshire stoneware teapots on display and one of the smallest teapots was of a rare Glasgow early 19th-century make.

Various institutions had their own pavilions, *The Times*, the British Broadcasting Corporation, ICI and the Dunlop Rubber Company among them. There were some broadcasts from Bellahouston but not enough to please the newspaper critics, although outside broadcasting was still a comparative rarity. Nonetheless, by 1938 the great set pieces – the Boat Race, the Cup Final, Test Matches, the Derby, Coronations and State Funerals – had all been done and it is perhaps a trifle surprising that more was not made of the international opportunity offered.

The Palace of Engineering was the largest, as befitted a region which had always specialised in heavy industry since the introduction of the factory system. It had been built by Sir William Arrol and Company and in its construction 1200 tons of steel had been used. It was here that such industrial giants as John Brown's displayed the models of the ships which had made them famous, the *Queen Mary*, the *Queen*

OVERTURE AND BEGINNERS

Elizabeth and the world's largest warship, HMS *Hood*. The latter was to be blown out of the water by the German battleship *Bismarck* within four years and of her crew of almost 1400 only three would survive the explosion in her magazine.

Such gloomy events were for the future and no pavilion attracted more attention than that of the Post Office, daringly and innovatively painted bright red. The feature was the model aeroplane which actually flew round the walls to indicate the principal air routes and by pressing a button the visitor could find out the exact air mail time between Great Britain and any part of the Empire. At this time the delivery of air mail was making extremely rapid progress with the pickaback planes, Mercury and Maia, being used for the transport of mail across the North Atlantic. The Post Office Pavilion was fiercely criticised as cheap and garish, but attracted large crowds with its models of cable-laying ships and of Mount Pleasant sorting office, while its stamp displays included Penny Blacks.

There was a Church of Scotland Pavilion and a Roman Catholic Pavilion, a Colville's Pavilion (steel was enormously important still) and a Coal Pavilion. A competition was held, a beauty competition of sorts, to find two girls who would act as the Spirit of Coal, but with commendable thrift the still privately-run industry also wanted them to act as usherettes. There was no lack of things to do or see. Who could ask for anything more?

The United Kingdom Pavilion, designed by Herbert Rowse.

CHAPTER FIVE
OFF AND RUNNING
EARLY DAYS AND ATTITUDES

ATTITUDES in Britain towards the Empire had not significantly changed in the course of the 20th century. There had been no relinquishing of territory and indeed some had come the way of Britain after 1918 in the allocation of mandated German colonies. Britain did not own them, true, but she had the responsibility for administering them. The white dominions, though there were stirrings here and there, seemed firmly within the Empire or Commonwealth, a new word which had gained ground since the passing of the Statute of Westminster in 1931. Even South Africa, which might legitimately be thought to be most at risk, seemed snugly within the Imperial fold as long as General Smuts was in charge. Smuts was extremely popular in this country for he conformed to the great Imperial stereotype of the defeated foe who had seen the light and lived to serve the conqueror loyally.

Partly because of political upheaval and defeat, partly because of the religious wars of the 17th-century and their repercussions, partly because of the poverty of the country which impelled many Scots to seek a living abroad and more especially when this natural process was accelerated by the Highland Clearances, Scots had always played a disproportionate part in the establishment of Empire. In India, the Marquis of Dalhousie had exercised a beneficent sway, while the great explorers David Livingstone and Mungo Park had mapped out much of unknown Africa. Their counterpart in Canada had been Alexander MacKenzie, while in Australia Lachlan Macquarie had been the visionary fifth Governor of New South Wales who said and believed that convicts were capable of redemption, and in the same colony John Macarthur defied the derision of the know-alls to introduce the Merino sheep which were to transform the economy of the new settlement.

THE EMPIRE EXHIBITION OF 1938

It is easy today to forget how recent much of the work of the settlement and development still was in 1938. There were visitors to the Exhibition who had very much been part of those early years. One of them was the daughter of David Livingstone, Mrs Livingstone Wilson, who came to Bellahouston at the age of 79. Naturally she was taken to see the model of those Victoria Falls which her father had named and she pronounced the miniature to be a marvellous achievement. "The only thing I missed looking at them today was the ground reverberations which one feels so strongly alongside the original falls." Interestingly Mrs Livingstone Wilson revealed that as a child she preferred to play with her uncle rather than with the stern and austere father whom of course she saw comparatively seldom.

Modern transport developments seemed to be making the Empire stronger. If Mrs Livingstone Wilson had wished, she could have flown to and from South Africa in 12 days. The overall attitude of those who favoured the Empire was still inevitably paternalistic. The opponents of Empire, and on the left they were many, weakened their case by failing to realise the genuine concern and intensive labour with which many of the workers in the imperial vineyards discharged their tasks.

The Empire's supporters, however, almost without exception and even if subconsciously, were like fathers whose children will never grow up but remain in a state of perpetual tutelage, at least so far as the non-white territories were concerned. This impression was reinforced by boys' books, songs and films. The native population made loyal soldiers when well commanded, loveable if eccentric servants, treacherous enemies when suborned from their allegiance to the great white father. The hero types were Gunga Din, the loyal Askaris in *Sanders of the River*, Pieter Pienaar, the Boer who had come to see the error of his ways in John Buchan's later books.

John Buchan in fact came to the Exhibition though by this time he was Lord Tweedsmuir and for him the imperial wheel had turned the full geographical and career cycle. Beginning as one of Milner's Young Men in South Africa, following the Boer War (he had been part of what we would today call a think-tank) he was ending his days as Governor-General of Canada. He had written *Prester John*, possibly the best-ever novel set in the Empire, and it is of no use to blame him because its attitudes and therefore his were those of his time. Good natives helped

OFF AND RUNNING—EARLY DAYS AND ATTITUDES

The Tourism and Travel Pavilion with a tower suggestive of a lighthouse.

the British, those who fought against them were not freedom campaigners in the style of the 1980s but ungrateful traitors who must be suppressed ruthlessly.

It followed therefore that there were certain ambiguities and uncertainties in the treatment of those coloured fellow-citizens of Empire who came to Glasgow in 1938. The unspoken assumption was that whites would travel to a predominantly white event. Few of the hotels in Glasgow would accept coloured guests and even fewer were open about this bar. On 2 June a Scottish woman missionary complained that she and an African colleague had been refused service in the Atlantic Restaurant, the most prestigious of the Exhibition restaurants and the one to which the King and Queen had been taken on opening day. The manager denied that

THE EMPIRE EXHIBITION OF 1938

this had happened but as he also denied that they had any coloured visitors since opening day the worth of his asseveration may be judged by that. Not the least of the problems surrounding the engagement of Paul Robeson, the famous negro bass singer, was to find accommodation for him that would at least be commensurate in part with his rating as a world star.

All that is not to be critical of the British Empire in isolation. Robeson would have experienced the same problems in even greater degree in at least half-a-dozen of the southern states in his own country. It served to reveal however, one of the myths which surrounded the mystique of Empire and by which it had been sustained, to wit, that any citizen of the Empire could travel freely within its bounds. The unspoken assumption had been that it would only be white citizens who would have the means or inclination to do this. No amount of disinterested and even generous government could disguise from the subject peoples the fact that they were deemed inferior, lesser breeds even if within the law, in contradiction of Kipling's phrase. This would be a major reason why the shy, dutiful man who had just opened the Empire Exhibition would be the last King-Emperor.

The Exhibition was an obvious platform from which to sell the idea of overseas resettlement and while there was not an inordinate amount of drum-beating, there was some. Organisations such as the British League of Empire were extremely anxious to encourage emigration to the Dominions and they would have approved of the speech of Viscount Horne of Slamannan. Lord Horne said, "A redistribution of population within the Empire is vital both for purposes of development and defence."

These views were reinforced by Vice-Admiral E.A. Taylor MP when he alluded to the consequences of any failure to populate vacant cultivable areas with people of British stock. "The only alternative is to have an ever-increasing population of foreign nationals settling there, nationals who in so many instances have not the same democratic outlook, the same mentality or the same ideals of language." Presumably by the last phrase he meant that Greeks and Italians had an unfortunate habit of speaking Greek and Italian.

Some of the Colonies were likewise in the business of attraction. There is a special irony in the appeal from the Southern Rhodesian (Zimbabwean) High Commissioner for families to settle there with a view to tobacco-growing. No tax was payable on incomes below £800 per annum and even then only 6d in the pound

OFF AND RUNNING—EARLY DAYS AND ATTITUDES

THE WOOL PAVILION, one of many devoted to specific crops or products.

on the next £500. Even today there may well be people in what once was Southern Rhodesia worried beyond measure over their future safety, growing a crop which increasingly the Western world rejects and in a perilous economic and political situation because their fathers or grandfathers responded to just such an offer in 1938.

These problems were for the future. In the meantime people flocked from all parts of Scotland and further away to see the recreations of those lands which they had only heard about in missionary sermons or read of in the pages of boys' magazines. Only the occasional whimsical note introduced a touch of discord, as in this tongue-in-cheek offering by Simplicitas in the *Evening Times:* "The character of the Empire's inhabitants in general is high. Quite 80 million are Christians and the rest are benefited by contact. Even those who are not Christians are often English-speaking so that altogether the people of the Empire form a great force for good. One may contrast the Roman Empire which consisted largely of heathens speaking Latin or Greek." Almost everyone reading that in 1938 would have taken it at face value.

There were problems to be resolved nearer home. The Exhibition was off to a brisk start, but from the point of view of the guarantors Sunday opening might well make all the difference to the financial position at the end of the run. For a time it seemed as if this might well come about, and indeed there had been a late attempt in April to ensure that at least the educational sections should be open. It was never seriously proposed to open the Amusement Park or the livelier forms of concert entertainment.

City Treasurer Patrick Dollan argued fiercely for Sunday opening. He pointed out that in its absence many working men would in effect be excluded from the teaching possibilities of the great show, and that the opponents of Sunday opening had been strangely muted in the Spring months when it was well known that considerable Sunday overtime was being worked on the site. Lord Weir and Sir James Lithgow associated themselves with these remarks. Sunday opening however foundered on the opposition of the Church of Scotland. This had been best expressed on the day before the Exhibition opened in an appeal signed by Lord Kinnaird, Lord High Commissioner to the General Assembly in 1937, and the Very Revd Dugald MacFarlane of Edinburgh Presbytery, the originators of the petition:

"No British Exhibition has ever opened on Sundays and the traditions of many generations cry out against it . . . For high and holy reasons they [*the organisers*] should abide by their former decision and disregard this late-hour proposal."

However reluctantly, the organisers did exactly that, saving face a little by stating that the problems of catering for the large crowds expected on Sundays were insuperable. From time to time during the run of the Exhibition, as the international situation and the dreadful weather affected attendances, there would be attempts to revive the question of Sunday opening, but in the end the Sabbatarians prevailed.

On the question of the nude statues Mrs Grundy had the last word. These were modern statues of nubile young women in a state of nature which had been put up without any great outcry, but within a few days of the opening they had been distinguished as a threat to the morals of visitors. Opinion in the letters column of the *Evening Times* was evenly divided between those who saw this as exactly

The Times Pavilion. The Times Newspaper carried enormous weight at this period because of its utterances on such topics as the Abdication and Munich. It provided one of the most distinctive buildings of the Exhibition.

THE EMPIRE EXHIBITION OF 1938

THE GLASGOW HERALD PAVILION. *In 1938 Glasgow still had three evening papers, each of which sold over 150,000 nightly.*

the kind of lascivious happening they had always known would come in the wake of the Exhibition and those who thought that the objectors were merely making themselves ridiculous on an even more exposed platform than usual.

Most bizarre of the letters was the one which made the following proposal in the *Evening Times*: "All the naked statues could be provided quite cheaply with little tartan kilts which would at once serve the purposes of decency and be a helpful advertisement for Scotland . . . This is a country where nudity is not practicable."

OFF AND RUNNING—EARLY DAYS AND ATTITUDES

GENERAL VIEW of Dominion Avenue. Note the boy with delivery bike in the foreground.

So propriety and financial acumen went happily hand-in-hand into the sunset, but on the questions of bars the sinners eventually carried the day. At first there had been only table licences and the Labour members of Glasgow Town Council quite properly pointed out that this weighed heavily against the working man who could not afford to patronise the Bellahouston restaurants. Even in those restaurants there was for the first few weeks no Saturday lunchtime licence, a carry-over from those recent days when working men were paid on a Saturday morning and all too many of them had squandered their week's wages before they ever saw home. Eventually, of the 16 restaurants and cafés at Bellahouston, seven were licensed in some form or other.

By the end of the first month there was much to praise, but various weaknesses had been identified and some constructive suggestions could be made. The major defects were perceived to be the following:

1. There were too few restaurants, teabars, tearooms and bars.
2. There should be half-price for children in the tearooms (a surprising omission on the face of it).
3. There should be no separate charge for the Palace of Arts.
4. The parking fee of one shilling was too high.
5. There should be more seats in the avenues.
6. There should be Sunday opening.

The last proposal was not entertained but most of the other objections were met at least in part. Refreshment tents were set up and, as a newspaper columnist rather patronisingly wrote, "The marquees have proved of great benefit to working class people who have not previously been able to get a bite of food." The *de haut en bas* tone should not obscure the truth of the statement. Original lunch prices had ranged from 1/6d to 6/6d, and in certain circumstances in the Atlantic Restaurant a visitor might pay 12/6d. Such prices were far beyond the range of the working man and his family and even the 1/- to 3/- demanded for the traditional "high tea" could not easily be found when a man in work did well to earn £3 a week.

None of this should detract from the undoubted fact that the Exhibition was a distinct success. The one-millionth visitor was recorded on 14 May, even although the weather showed prolonged and ominous signs of worsening. There was great excitement every time the "Empirex", as it was almost universally known, seemed on the point of reaching another million visitors. All the gates were sealed off save a couple for the officials to announce with a wavering degree of certainty who the last person through the turnstile had been. The chosen one was usually given free passes and a special tour of the site. By a fair bit of judicious manipulation Her Royal Highness Princess Elizabeth was officially declared to be the ten-millionth visitor when she came north in September.

The Canadian Pavilion.

Palace of Engineering. One of the few buildings to survive the Exhibition it was relocated at Prestwick by Scottish Aviation. Note the Lister auto truck in the foreground. These were used to take visitors round the Exhibition grounds.

Dominion Avenue. This view of the Dominion and Irish Pavilions also affords a clear idea of what a Danish architect called the "daemonic verticality" of the Tower of Empire.

North Cascade and Tower. The Church of Scotland Pavilion is on the left. Note that although the day is fine and canny Glaswegians have happed up well.

The Lake Fountains. The "dancing fountains" were one of the great attractions of the Exhibition, especially at night when they changed colour bewilderingly. The water spectacle at Bellahouston was on a scale never attempted before or since in Britain.

The Atlantic Restaurant. Built in the form of the bows of a ship it was staffed by ships' stewards and was the most impressive and expensive of the restaurants. The round glass-fronted building is the BBC Pavilion with the Scottish Pavilion (South) in the left background.

Bandstand. One of the two bandstands which were used for concerts during the Exhibition and, in the later stages, for outdoor dancing. The Palace of Industries is in the background.

Another view of the Bandstand and Tower. The Glasgow Herald *Pavilion is on the lower left.*

Scottish Avenue. The two Scottish Pavilions are at the end of the avenue with Ibrox Stadium the home of Rangers FC beyond them on the left. The ever-present industrial haze covers the city.

The Clachan. This idealised reconstruction of a Highland hamlet proved very popular with overseas visitors and oddly enough, with Highlanders. The gangway provided a particularly vivid reminder of Western Isles holidays for many who came.

The Clachan. Another view of The Clachan and its administrative staff.

The Loch that never was. A cunningly-painted backcloth lent the impression of a distant sea vista from The Clachan.

Ordinary visitors. There was always a queue of people waiting to buy postcards of The Clachan and send them from the little Post Office.

Distinguished visitors. King George VI, Queen Elizabeth and the Earl of Elgin visit the Post Office in the Clachan on the official opening day of the Empire Exhibition of 1938.

CHAPTER SIX
MR BUTLIN'S PLEASURE-DOME

IN setting up the Exhibition and considering its attractions the Executive were very conscious of the fact that each of the previous events in Glasgow, although all had shown a profit, had been criticised for not providing enough in the way of entertainment for the ordinary man and his family and it was therefore determined that this should not in 1938 be a cause for complaint.

There was certainly a need for leavening, because even although the organisers were well aware of the need for "innocent merriment" the countervailing forces had already organised, as was noted in City and Clyde, the diary column of the *Evening Times:* "Visitors entering the Exhibition by the turnstiles at the North-East gates must wonder what they are walking into. Two of the earliest stands they see are emblazoned with Biblical texts, then come the stands of a tract society and of the Theosophists. On the left appears the Peace Pavilion and through the trees is the outline of a church. By this time, the visitors should indeed feel that 'life is real, life is earnest'."

It was agreed that a feature of the Empire Exhibition should be a large Amusement Park and initially the franchise was offered to the Green family, well-known among Scottish showmen. Native caution impelled them to turn it down however. The site was well away from the centre of Glasgow and Sunday opening, which would certainly have made the proposition extremely attractive, was out of the question. Even when the advocates of Sunday opening for the Exhibition seemed about to get their way, their case was only based on "those educational aspects of the great event". The Greens therefore quietly declined.

In their stead came a confident young Canadian, Billy Butlin, who would shortly

THE EMPIRE EXHIBITION OF 1938

become world-famous as the man whose name was synonymous with holiday camps, and who could indeed be fairly regarded as the pioneer of holidays in the mass. He had applied himself closely to the study of the psychology of crowds and he was happy to assume responsibility for the 16 acres of the 173 which had been allotted to diversion and jollity. One of his favourite sayings was that "it takes five grown-ups to take one child to the fair" and it was from the grown-ups that the fairground owners made their money.

Throughout the duration of the Exhibition the Amusement Park co-existed uneasily with the Trade and Industrial Pavilions and perhaps even more uneasily with the competing forms of entertainment, the bands, the variety artistes and the serious musicians. The orthodox exhibitors felt that the sideshows and roundabouts detracted from the primary purpose of an international trade fair. The serious musicians complained about the noise. Billy Butlin complained that when there was a particularly attractive variety act, such as Jack Hylton's band, the spectators deserted the Amusement Park in droves, especially when such bands gave *impromptu* open-air gratis performances. More than any other section of the Exhibition the fairground suffered from the appalling weather and there were grey evenings of drenching rain when it presented a bedraggled and dismal appearance.

The *Glasgow Herald* was massively unsympathetic to the plaints of the showmen who were after all paying heavy rents. It dismissed the protests of the stall-owners who complained about the open air dancing thus: "It is really most inconsiderate of the management to allow the public to find out what it wants, and then to go and supply it, when there are shooting galleries and dart boards and places for throwing money away there, ready and willing to provide the minimum of reward for the maximum of outlay. One would almost think that the Exhibition was being run for the enjoyment of the visitors."

For most of the time of course it was a very cheerful place. It offered an intriguing mixture of the tried standbys of fairgrounds, together with a collection of ultra-modern "stunts" as the new devices were called. Thus there was the Magic Carpet, which in other days would have been a simple Helter-Skelter, there was the Hall of Mirrors and the Crazy House where floors tilted under your feet and attractive young women found their skirts around their necks to the great delight of the spectators and to remarkably little embarrassment from themselves. Such at least must be the judgement since many of them paid repeat visits. There was a miniature

General view of The Amusement Park.

railway where the trains chugged sedately round the perimeter of the Amusement Park at an ambling eight miles an hour or so and yet provided one of the Exhibition's serious accidents. On 21 May the two trains collided, injuring 20 people of whom three had to be taken to hospital. The accident was due to simple human error; the railway was single-track most of the way and one of the drivers had simply forgotten to collect the key which acted as clearance to enter a particular section.

Great care had been taken to test the new attractions for safety. The quite terrifying scenic railway which had been tried by loading a car with sandbags to a weight greatly in excess of anything it was ever likely to carry, attained a top speed of 60

THE EMPIRE EXHIBITION OF 1938

One of the model engines arriving for the miniature railway in the Amusement Park.

miles-an-hour and proved extremely popular with the Glaswegians and those from further afield. It was sampled by some rather exalted visitors—the Moderator of the General Assembly of the Church of Scotland, the Right Reverend James Black, rode the track and pronounced, "Well, that was grand." Even greater dignitaries followed him. In August the Duke and Duchess of Gloucester experienced its delights and those of the petrol-driven speedway cars for good measure. The correct title for the speedway cars was the Brooklands Racer, where although the cars only attained a top speed of 20 miles an hour, the small wheels and miniature steering-wheel gave the illusion of motor racing.

Man's conquest of the air was reflected in many of the amusements. There were

MR BUTLIN'S PLEASURE-DOME

View of the formidable scenic railway.

Loop O' Planes which were a development of the old Steamboats and which eventually swung themselves up until they described complete circles. The Stratoplane did this too but had other interesting gyrations in store for those intrepid enough to try it. Popular too was the Rise to Heaven which consisted of a huge tower with a massive cross-bar at the top. Two globes, each containing 20 people were hauled up to the end of each arm of the bar and the great attraction of this ride was that the globes spun and swayed in the wind.

The Amusement Park also boasted the largest Dodg'em track in the world, occupying an entire acre. On the Dodg'em track small cars, electrically powered and equipped with heavy rubber bumpers, smashed into each other with cheerful

THE EMPIRE EXHIBITION OF 1938

PAY ON THE PLANE. *The hobby-horse was giving way to the fighter plane.*

abandon. There was even a Dodg'em Lake where small motor boats did the same and this was vastly popular. In a huge tank of water the boats caromed off each other as their tall pennons struck sparks from the roof of the booth. This maritime carnage was presided over by the Admiral of the Dodg'ems, majestic in thigh boots and sailor's jersey as he separated the interlocked boats. To a child he was power and romance incarnate and although he may well have detested what he was doing his job was certainly the first ever coveted by many a small visitor.

Many of the staff at the Amusement Park hated not so much what they were doing as how long they were expected to do it for. Trade Union leaders complained that casual workers were being required to work 15 to 16 hours per day without

Space travel was a prominent theme of the Exhibition Fairground.

anything in the way of provision of lavatories and rest-rooms. There were mutterings about the prices of the roundabouts, sixpence and a shilling a time being thought rather steep, but Butlin countered with the riposte that there was not a range of entertainments like this anywhere in the world.

There were also sideshows. The giraffe-necked women were featured in the sideshow rather inaccurately called Savage West Africa and great play was made with the fact that they had to go to the baths in Paisley each week to perform ceremonial ablutions. Later in the Exhibition one of the women gave birth but at least her offspring appears to have been spared the donation of a hideously inappropriate first name, unlike the hapless Waverley Mamadou Diop from 1911. To balance the tall dusky women there were midgets from France and Poland in another booth.

Some things were too bizarre for even Mr Butlin to countenance. A young man, Eric Selwyn, offered to be buried alive for a protracted period as a "stunt". Through a shaft in the covering earth visitors would be able to look down at his glass-fronted coffin. Always mindful of the fact that he was providing an entertainment and wishing to give value for money, Mr. Selwyn proposed to equip his coffin with both telephone and microphone so that he could give commentaries on his macabre experience. Selwyn was extremely put out when Mr Butlin declined to entertain his suggestion and appealed unsuccessfully against this decision to the Administrative Committee. Fortunately for Mr Selwyn the magistrates of Great Yarmouth proved to be more accommodating and he was able to perform his weird feat of endurance in the English resort shortly afterwards.

The showmen too were baffled and sometimes irked by what they saw as unnecessary limitations on their attempts to attract customers. On 8 July they were forbidden in their role as barkers to use hand-microphones as there had been complaints from trade exhibitors and musicians. The fairground people were not used to this kind of competition in the normal run of things. The Laughing Sailor who guffawed continuously above the Crazy House was exempted from the ban.

There were accidents, for not every piece of equipment could be guaranteed against the high spirits and occasional intoxication of the visitors. The most serious accident occurred in the very first week when four young men began to clown while at the top of The Big Wheel. One was thrown out and sustained serious injuries, from which he subsequently died. Perhaps sympathy might be better reserved for Mrs Annie Watson or Cook, from Ayr, who was strolling peacefully through the grounds when the head fell off the Laughing Sailor and struck her to her considerable bruising and shock.

Billy Butlin was in the classical tradition of showmen who gave the public what it wants by guiding it in the direction of what it should want. He had studied his market. In an interview of the time it was suggested that the more frightening of

MR BUTLIN'S PLEASURE-DOME

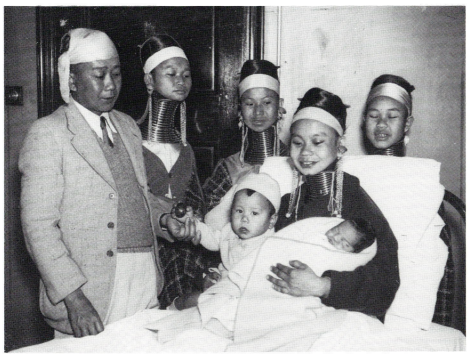

Proud Parents. One of the giraffe-necked women gave birth to a daughter during the Empire Exhibition.

his attractions would be almost exclusively patronised by young men seeking to impress their girlfriends with their courage. He disagreed. "It is women who like such sideshows as the Loop O' Plane. Women like to be looked at. Men don't. A crowd gathers all the time the Loop O' Plane is working. It's simple psychology. Women buy weird hats and want to be in the limelight. When I want to buy a hat I go in and buy one exactly like my last one . . . That's why 75 per cent of the people who go on exciting stunts are women."

Things picked up for the showmen when for the last two months of the Exhibition they were allowed to stay open until midnight on three midweek evenings and on Saturdays, although this concession was offset to some degree by the truly appalling weather which characterised the closing stages. This caused problems for

THE EMPIRE EXHIBITION OF 1938

some of the more daring artistes who performed extremely risky individual acts. One such was Camille Mayer of Harrisburg, Pennsylvania. Billed as the Stratosphere Girl, she performed acrobatics on a metal wheel at the top of a metal mast 137 feet high. Her act was certainly risky and she was extremely popular, her engagement being extended, but a few months later the newspapers carried reports of her death in Germany while performing there.

Slightly more fortunate was Daredevil Peggy whose name was Frank C. Gadsby. His odd title did not refer to any sexual ambiguity as it might today but rather to the fact that he had only one leg. His act involved him in diving 75 feet into a pool which had been set alight and on one occasion both his cloak and the pool itself caught fire to a greater degree than had been intended. The Gadsby family did not seem blessed by fortune for another member, Leslie, who had only one hand was blown by a high wind from the platform as he was about to dive 20 feet into a tank.

Exactly one year before the outbreak of war it was proposed that the site should become permanent and house a huge Amusement Park or Zoo. The worsening situation internationally put paid to this as it did to all plans for permanent location but the Amusements at the Empire Exhibition had given great delight and formed for many people their abiding impression of it and one which solaced them in the bitter days ahead.

CHAPTER SEVEN
SPORT AT THE EMPIRE EXHIBITION

THE fact that there was one of the most modern football grounds in Britain on the very doorstep of Bellahouston Park had not escaped the notice of those who felt that the event ought to be commemorated by one or more professional sporting tournaments. Of the sports envisaged, Association football was clearly the one which had the best chance of being successful in terms of financial return. Scotland's devotion to the game was deep-rooted and almost insatiable and within Scotland, Glaswegians stood pre-eminent in their fervour.

To mark the fact that the Exhibition was one for the whole of Britain, though located in Scotland, it was thought appropriate that an Anglo-Scottish football tournament should be held, involving four of the leading clubs from each country. This would give an unusual dimension to the competition and to further stress the Exhibition connection, the trophy that was to be played for would be very special. It was to take the form of a replica of the Exhibition Tower, and was to be of silver, 18 inches high and based on a suitable plinth. With the Glasgow Merchants Charity Cup as its only rival, the Exhibition Trophy may fairly claim to be the most beautiful in all football.

Members of the winning side would receive a silver miniature of this trophy and all other competing teams would receive a similar miniature but in plate. To mark his energetic efforts in staging the Exhibition, the trophy would be presented to the winning captain after the final match by the Earl of Elgin.

Glasgow could in the 1930s fairly claim to be the world capital of Association football. It possessed two grounds, Hampden Park and Ibrox, on which last the Exhibition Trophy matches would be played, which could and had held crowds of

THE EMPIRE EXHIBITION OF 1938

considerably more than 100,000. Indeed in the previous year, on successive Saturdays, crowds of 149,000 and 146,000 had been recorded for the international match against England and the Scottish Cup final. If one adds to this the fact that Celtic Park could hold 90,000 spectators and that there were three other major football grounds in Glasgow, of which the smallest held 30,000, then some notion may be gained of the city's prodigious appetite for this particular ball game.

As with every other aspect of the Exhibition there were the doubters and the prophets of doom. It was suggested that the weather might be too hot for top-class football (a remote contingency in the normal Scottish summer). Would not the competing sides be stale after a nine-month long league campaign? Nor did the selection of the four English sides cause universal satisfaction. Arsenal and Manchester City had been invited and had both declined. These were serious losses in that Arsenal were certainly the most publicised team of the time and were already well-known in Scotland by virtue of a series of annual friendly matches which they had begun to play against Rangers. There had even been a film made about them, *The Arsenal Stadium Mystery*, a British "B" movie in which a crime story was located within Arsenal's ground at Highbury in North London.

Manchester City would have arrived as a Second Division team but a most quixotically attractive one for all that. They had just achieved the unusual distinction of having been relegated to the Second Division although scoring more goals than any other side in the First Division, which they had just left. A free-scoring forward line was continually betrayed by a leaky defence and City left the upper echelons of footballing society. They would have been a considerable draw and their loss was grievous. Aston Villa, who might have provided a very acceptable substitute, were engaged on a Continental tour of Germany and Austria, or of Greater Germany since the Anschluss of March 1938 had made the former distinction redundant.

At the end of the day the flag of England was borne by Everton, Sunderland who had won the FA Cup in the previous year, 1937, Chelsea and Brentford. The last named team may come as something of a surprise choice to those whose footballing memories begin with the 1950s. It is true that the post-war record of the West London club has been quite undistinguished but in the immediate pre-1939 years they were numbered among the top six sides in England.

The honour of Scotland would be defended by the two great Glasgow clubs,

SPORT AT THE EMPIRE EXHIBITION

The Rangers and Celtic teams of 1938 being shown over the Exhibition by Councillor Patrick Dollan, later Lord Provost of Glasgow.

Celtic and Rangers, the latter having the considerable advantage of playing on their home ground, to which were added Heart of Midlothian from Edinburgh and Aberdeen. All matches would be played at Ibrox Stadium with a seven p.m. kick-off and the draw and timetable turned out thus:

    25 May   Celtic v. Sunderland
    27 May   Aberdeen v. Chelsea
    30 May   Rangers v. Everton
    1 June   Heart of Midlothian v. Brentford.

THE EMPIRE EXHIBITION OF 1938

It will immediately be seen that the time-scale was very brief and the long early summer nights of Scotland were to be used if necessary in an attempt to gain a decision. There would be an extra 30 minutes played in the event of a draw over 90 minutes (a most unusual proceeding for the first match of a cup-tie in Scotland) and if the sides were still level at the end of two hours they would meet again the following evening and play to a finish no matter how long that might take.

This provision had to be invoked in the very first match of the tournament when in cool overcast weather with rainy showers (the tournament was blessed with that weather which although damaging to the main Exhibition was ideal for playing football), 55,000 people saw Celtic and Sunderland play out a goalless draw. The chief sports correspondent of the *Evening Times*, Archie Y. Wilson, who in the fashion of his day used the *nom-de-plume* of Alan Breck, was full of praise for the keenness with which both sides played. His only major reservation was that the price of the stand seats was much too high at 5/- for the centre stand and 3/6d for the inner wings.

Playing again the following evening as the rules of the competition decreed, Celtic came out victors by 3–1 and even on a very bad night 21,000 found a second sum of money for the match. There was clearly going to be a lot of money to be gained, for the competing clubs shared one-third of the gate after ground rent had been paid to Rangers and the Exhibition itself had received its share.

One Scottish club was therefore through to the semi-finals and it became two on the evening of 27 May when Aberdeen easily disposed of Chelsea 4–0. Whereas Sunderland's commitment had won high praise in the two matches they played, Chelsea were roundly condemned for the casual attitude which they displayed towards the competition and barbed remarks about the effete Southerners studded the commentaries of the sports reporters. The difference in approach was almost certainly not due to geographical location since, apart from anything else Chelsea like the other three participating English clubs had a considerable number of Anglo-Scots in their side. The average number of Scots playing in an English side over the tournament was four.

No, what almost certainly coloured Chelsea's approach which verged upon the lackadaisical and drew from the *Evening Times* the taunt "No wonder they are called the Pensioners!", was the knowledge that the rewards being paid to players were very dissimilar at an English and a Scottish level. Members of the Scottish

THE EMPIRE EXHIBITION TOURNAMENT. *This Anglo-Scottish football competition attracted huge crowds to Ibrox Park. Here Mapson, the Sunderland goalkeeper clears from Crum of Celtic who is on the ground. Celtic won the competition.*

THE EMPIRE EXHIBITION OF 1938

clubs were paid £5 per man per match irrespective of the result, while the English clubs were held to payments of £2 per match for a win and £1 for a draw. Not even the provision of ten shillings a day pocket money or the fact that they quartered well (Chelsea stayed at Turnberry and Everton at Skelmorlie Hydro) could induce the Londoners to stir themselves greatly and in view of the crowds attracted (there were more than 20,000 at the Chelsea game) it is very difficult to censure them too severely. They were grossly underpaid.

The matches were to be controlled both by English and by Scottish referees. If the final was played between two Scottish sides then Peter Craigmyle of Aberdeen would be in charge. If between two English entrants then Mr T. Thomson of Northumberland would officiate. If there was an Anglo-Scottish final the two gentlemen mentioned would draw lots and the winner would referee.

As yet the first round was not completed and the final some little way off, but the defeat of Rangers in the first round by Everton led to complaints about the different interpretation of the laws exercised by the English referee. Alan Breck would have none of it however: "Rangers were for me beaten by a better team and it is good to see that honest man-to-man charging still has a part to play in our national game."

The first round was completed when Brentford played by far the best football of the four English clubs and yet went out 1-0 to Hearts. The attendance for this match which had of course no direct Glasgow involvement reached a staggering 46,000 and already cries were heard for the tournament to become an annual event.

History was made, footballing history at any rate, when for the first of the semi-finals, an all-Scottish affair between Celtic and Hearts, an English referee, Dr A.W. Barton of Derby, was appointed. This was thought to have been the first time that a competitive match between Scottish clubs in Scotland had been controlled by an English referee. Just under 50,000 spectators saw Celtic go through economically to the final by a solitary goal. There they would meet English opposition for the other semi-final went in favour of Everton, who edged out Aberdeen narrowly by 3-2. The scorers in this match are of more than passing interest and offer a cameo insight of the game in the 1930s. Everton's goals fell to Boyes, an England international, Gillick, who had been with Rangers and would be with them again, and Tommy Lawton, the famous international centre-forward who had recently joined Everton from Burnley. Aberdeen's goals fell to their

More football action from the Exhibition. Cook of Everton (left) tussles with Strauss of Aberdeen for the ball.

long-serving centre-forward Matt Armstrong and to Billy Strauss, one of the surprisingly large number of South Africans who were playing professional football in Scotland at that time. After their success on the playing field the Everton team went dancing at the Exhibition and were photographed on the dance floor.

THE EMPIRE EXHIBITION OF 1938

All that was needed to set the absolute seal of success on the trophy was that it should be won by a Scottish club and this duly came to pass when on 10 June Celtic got the better of Everton, again by a solitary goal although the match had to go to extra time to produce a result. Their centre-forward Johnny Crum, who had scored the semi-final goal against Hearts was again their marksman. The Exhibition tournament had been an outstanding financial success. In weather which was never good and for two of the matches downright bad, 340,000 spectators in all had attended. The two finalists received £2,500 for their efforts and this at a time when £10,000 was regarded as a huge expenditure for the transfer of a player. The Exhibition funds themselves benefited to the extent of £4,250.

There were many and vociferous suggestions that the tournament must become an annual affair but they came to nothing. There were several impediments. Club sides were increasingly making tours of the Continent on their own account and international matches were growing in frequency. In those far-off days of the 1930s football sides were remarkably far-travelled. Confining instances to the Scottish game we find that in the previous ten years both Rangers and Celtic had been to Canada and the United States, Motherwell and Aberdeen to South Africa and even the comparatively unfashionable Queen of the South had been to North Africa and the South of France. There was thus the question of availability of the players. The outbreak of war the following year postponed any further thoughts of a follow-up almost indefinitely and it was not until the Coronation of Her Majesty Queen Elizabeth II that a similar competition was held, the Coronation Cup, with the venue this time being Hampden Park.

Strangely, despite the lapse of 15 years, a very long time in footballing terms, there were two players who took part in both competitions, one English, one Scottish. The Englishman was Joe Mercer who had changed by 1953 from the blue shirt of Everton to the red and white of Arsenal. The case of the Scot is even stranger. George Hamilton played for Aberdeen as a 20-year-old in 1938 and for the same club in 1953 as a grizzled veteran in his mid-thirties It may be worth adding that subsequent attempts to set up such Anglo-Scottish tournaments on an annual basis have all failed dismally. It would appear that one of the things required for their success is novelty, that in Shakespeare's phrase "When they seldom come, they wished-for come".

It had been an excellent competition, tightly run, and Glasgow in general and

SPORT AT THE EMPIRE EXHIBITION

Willie Lyon, captain of Celtic receives the Exhibition Trophy from the Earl of Elgin after his side had defeated Everton in the final at Ibrox Park.

Ibrox Stadium in particular had been seen to great advantage. In teeming rain the pitch itself had stood up to very heavy and intensive traffic. Ironically it was immediately to be subjected to traffic which it would find very difficult to withstand. The United Services Display, which was to be held at the Rangers' ground in

THE EMPIRE EXHIBITION OF 1938

conjunction with the Exhibition, had literally a cast of thousands. There were to be 10,000 troops, including mechanised cavalry, tanks and dispatch riders. To take the weight 20 blocks of concrete six feet square were sunk below various parts of the playing area but the drainage and the appearance of the pitch were severely affected and it would be many years before the playing surface of Ibrox Park returned to the standards of 1938.

Ibrox Stadium, though, was also the setting for another large-scale professional sporting event, this time in the shape of a tennis circus. A special wooden court was constructed in front of the main stand and on it four of the leading professional players of the day played a series of exhibition matches. In the years up until 1960 professional tennis players could make a reasonable income at top level but they earned it in a kind of limbo, cut off totally from the major championships such as Wimbledon and Forest Hills and condemned to an endless round of exhibition matches in which it was common knowledge that sets were "massaged" to ensure a best-of-three finish.

It had been hoped to bring Fred Perry to Ibrox, and as someone who had recently turned professional and as a Briton who had won Wimbledon in three consecutive years, he would have been a great attraction. He did not show, nor did the Frenchman Henri Cochet, one of the famous "Four Musketeers" of the marvellous French Davis Cup team of the 1920s. The only real name was Bill Tilden, of the ferocious service, and he was joined in the matches by Hans Nusslein of Germany and two French players, R. Ramillon and M. Plaa. The tournament took place at Ibrox from 5 July to 7 July but the tennis event which made the headlines on those days was the news of the death of Suzanne Lenglen, arguably the first person to introduce professional standards and values to women's tennis. She had revolutionised dress on court, trained harder than it had hitherto been considered seemly to do and in pursuit of her own standards of excellence had not scrupled to keep the Queen waiting her pleasure at Wimbledon. Now, at the sorrowfully early age of 39, she was dead of anaemia and her death did tend to overshadow the on-court events at Ibrox.

There were other sporting notables who came to the Empire Exhibition. The Australian touring cricket side of 1938 under Don Bradman came to Bellahouston while in Scotland to play a couple of matches. The Exhibition, on a grimmer note, witnessed almost the last appearance in public of one of Scotland's most popular

102

athletes, the boxer Benny Lynch. Having signed a contract for a world title flyweight match against Jackie Jurich of the United States, the two men visited the Exhibition after the formalities had been accomplished. The fight was due to take place at Love Street, Paisley, the home of St Mirren Football Club and within three miles of the Exhibition Grounds.

There had been increasingly strong rumours that Lynch, who had a past history of drinking problems, would find it difficult to make the weight but his camp stridently denied this and the little boxer was warmly welcomed as he was conducted on a tour of the Exhibition grounds. The rumours proved to be only too well founded when on the day of the fight, Lynch failed to make the weight by a matter of pounds rather than ounces and was stripped of his titles on the scales. It was not untypical that in the subsequent bout, fought at catchweights, he should box very well and get the better of a heavily outweighted Jurich but it was the end of his professional career. He did take part in one more fiasco of a contest in London but with the outbreak of war he fell into a penurious obscurity and died in grim circumstances at the end of hostilities, an end which was not the less distressing for being so predictable. Many saw him as the individual example of the Scottish experience, trying to fight his way out of a bleak, hopeless environment with only his will and raw courage for allies. Lynch had climbed to the edge of the pit only to topple back. Could his country make it to safety and prosperity?

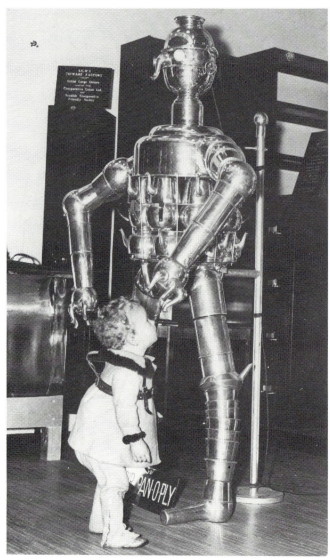

Tot meets robot. The impressive looking mechanical man is constructed entirely from pots and pans.

CHAPTER EIGHT
ORDINARY AND DISTINGUISHED VISITORS

PEOPLE came to the Exhibition by every form of transport. From the Clyde coast towns of Rothesay and Dunoon, paddle steamers made the voyage up the river to Broomielaw, reversing the usual process of river traffic by which scores of thousands of Glaswegians each summer went "doon the watter". At the beginning of June two small motor vessels, the *Ashton* and the *Leven*, began to make frequent daily trips from the Broomielaw down to John Brown's shipyard at Clydebank so that passengers could see the last stages in the fitting-out of the *Queen Elizabeth*, the huge Cunarder for whose launching the King and Queen would make a return visit to Scotland in September.

The great liners of the Anchor Donaldson fleet, the *Caledonia*, the *Cameronia*, the *Tuscania* and the *Transylvania*, brought returning exiled Scots from Canada and the United States of America to Yorkhill Quay, in the very centre of Glasgow. One of the Donaldson liners, the *Athenia*, would be the first merchant shipping casualty of World War Two on the first day of that conflict. Other visitors came from every part of Scotland by train, from the branch line which served the Kincardineshire towns of Inverbervie and Gourdon, from the West Highland line, from the main lines that ran south to the industrial North of England.

Glaswegians themselves crowded on to the modern tramcars which had been ordered for the twin occasions of the Coronation in 1937 and the Empire Exhibition the following year. The "new" trams would remain in service until the 1960s but never lost their tag of the Exhibition or Coronation trams. To add the proper note of festivity, all Corporation Transport Department employees whose routes took them to Bellahouston were required to wear white-topped caps which gave

THE EMPIRE EXHIBITION OF 1938

The four members of the Royal Canadian Mounted Police were a great draw. Here they make the acquaintaince of the 29th Company, Boys' Brigade.

them a smart summery appearance even if, all too often, the rainwater cascaded from their hats.

Large parties came to Bellahouston from England, co-operative societies, Vickers Armstrong and Lever Brothers among them. On August Bank Holiday 23 special trains brought no fewer than 17,000 visitors from the South. When schools restarted in August, Glasgow Corporation decided that it would foot the bill for 100,000 pupils to attend the Exhibition. The noted educationist Dr Maria Montessori declared that children should be allowed to wander the grounds on their own but this was not the Scottish way of doing things and many schools would

ORDINARY AND DISTINGUISHED VISITORS

John Buchan, Lord Tweedsmuir, the famous Scottish author places a stone on the Peace Cairn watched by Lady Aberdeen and Lord Elgin.

not even allow their charges to visit the Amusement Park after the serious work of sight-seeing had been done.

The problem of transporting visitors within the grounds themselves was solved brilliantly by the introduction of some 50 autotrucks, made by R.A. Lister and Company of Dursley in Gloucestershire. There were hard-working little trucks, capable of taking about 20 people at a time, on which passengers sat back to back something in the fashion of an Irish jaunting car. On average they covered 26 miles a day and took about 35 minutes to travel the longest distance between two points

THE EMPIRE EXHIBITION OF 1938

in the Exhibition, some two-and-a-half miles. Their pace was deliberately set at that of a brisk walk as the idea was that passengers could hop on and off while the auto-truck was in motion. They were not licensed to be driven on normal roads and when the Exhibition came to an end, they had to be loaded on to container lorries for the return trip to Gloucestershire. In concept and execution they were well ahead of their time and something along those lines would have provided a ready-made solution of the problem of transporting visitors from the entrance to Pollok Estate to the building which houses the Burrell Collection when eventually that was opened almost half a century later.

Early in July the truckmen staged the most effective strike the Exhibition was to experience when they struck for and obtained an increase in wages of five shillings per week. This victory raised the wages of a driver to £3–5s per week and those of a conductor to £3 per week.

The Royal Family continued to patronise the Exhibition faithfully. Princess Mary, the Princess Royal, came up to Glasgow but it was observed somewhat disapprovingly that "she went round in an awful rush". In late June the Duke of Gloucester visited the Exhibition with his wife Alice, who was of course Scottish, being a member of the family of Montague Douglas Scotts of Buccleuch. Onlookers exclaimed that the Duke appeared "animated and exhilarated". The following day his brother, Prince George, Duke of Kent, came to Bellahouston, accompanied by his very popular wife Princess Marina who was regarded as something of a trendsetter in fashion in the middle 1930s, especially in the matter of hats.

The most enthusiastic member of the House of Windsor where the Exhibition was concerned was undoubtedly Queen Mary. She had long been a revered figure but perceived as being extremely formal and rigid, a stickler for the stifling etiquette of the Court. It now appeared that since the death of her husband George V in January 1936 she had reverted somewhat to the more carefree attitudes of her youth. As the Exhibition ran its course she evinced a keener and keener interest in it, returning on three separate occasions in less than a week in September. At times she showed herself positively skittish. Charles Oakley remembers her demonstrating to a group of fascinated officials the correct way to do the steps of the Highland Fling.

She visited the Empire Cinema where she was fascinated by a Charlie Chaplin film, *The Champion*, and insisted on viewing it several times in succession. She

ORDINARY AND DISTINGUISHED VISITORS

Queen Mary was a frequent and perceptive visitor to the Exhibition and was particularly warm in its praise.

took over a simulator at a Corporation bus-driving school in the Glasgow Pavillion and proceeded to demolish buildings and other vehicles with a happy abandon. "You've smashed the bus!" shouted the Countess of Athlone, her lady-in-waiting with patrician glee. She also showed herself to be astonishingly perceptive. In the City of Glasgow Pavilion she was shown one of the first slum clearance plans for the city by the understandably proud councillors and officials. Her rejoinder was amazingly far-sighted: "What a pity many of the old houses can't be reconditioned as their walls are so much stouter than those of today." She had unerringly

THE EMPIRE EXHIBITION OF 1938

identified the course of action which, taken 40 years and five disastrous giant housing schemes later, would eventually prove to be both the salvation and the rejuvenation of what was proudly called in 1938 The Second City of the Empire.

Nobody who visited Bellahouston Park could fail to catch the palpable spirit of excitement that permeated the place. These new buildings were the way the future was going to look. These light and airy structures which looked more like glasshouses than factories would house the new light industries of the future. That there was a clamant need for Central Scotland to change industrial course could not be remotely doubted. It had to be weaned from its traditional total dependence on heavy industries – ships, locomotives, bridges, iron, coal – where either the raw materials were in process of being worked out or foreign competition was eroding our seniority and technical skills. Scotland was building up-to-date industrial estates such as Hillington which had a good infrastructure. It was vital that new firms should be attracted.

Two developments had caused the guarantors some slight uneasiness before the month of May was out. The Exhibition had been handicapped right at the start by a bus strike which for a few days paralysed Central Scotland. A leader article in the *Evening Times*, under the byline of Hal o' the Wynd, exhibited the lack of sympathy for the strikers which characterised most newspaper writing of the time. He was forthright in his condemnation: "I want to ask all you people who are involved in this strike, or likely to be involved in it, if you think your affairs are more important than the welfare of the Empire? By 'you people' I mean employers and employees in this and similar transport strikes. And by 'welfare of the Empire' I mean the immediate success of the Exhibition as a magnet for bringing the Empire together and pointing it to prosperity."

The other complaint was that the Exhibition was being inadequately publicised, especially in London which has never been celebrated for noticing greatly events which take place outwith the boundaries of that city. The Treasurer of Glasgow, Patrick Dollan, voiced his exasperation at a meeting of Glasgow Publicity Club the week after Their Majesties had declared the Exhibition open. He said: "Until it was opened by the King and Queen I am sure that many people in the South of England thought that it was being held in the Kelvin Hall and that visitors would have to walk three miles for a bottle of beer."

Even in this gloomy statement the City Treasurer was being over-optimistic, as

ORDINARY AND DISTINGUISHED VISITORS

the vast majority of the citizens of the South-East of England had never heard of the Kelvin Hall. The charge of lack of publicity was substantiated from an unexpected source, the Lord Mayor of London, no less. The Lord Mayor, Sir Harry Twyford, drove from the centre of Glasgow in the state coach which he used in the Lord Mayor's Show and he was accompanied by Mr Herbert Morrison, then leader of London County Council and subsequently a Cabinet Minister in the Attlee administration of 1945. London's leading citizen expressed himself delighted with what he had seen and promised to boost the Exhibition on his return to London, adding: "The only thing I regret is that more has not been told the English people, and particularly the London people, about the Exhibition."

By the early autumn the London Midland and Scottish Railway Company were running special weekend excursion trains from the capital, but it is hard to resist the conclusion that this strategy might well have been instituted earlier and prosecuted more vigorously.

No more than anywhere else could what was on offer at Bellahouston please all the people all the time. Long queues formed to listen to the Speaking Clock which had started in Scotland as a GPO service on 1 May. Even longer queues snaked round the United Kingdom Pavilion for a glimpse of the Mechanical Man, the Marvel of the Age. This was a working model of the upper half of the human body – a fortunate decision given the fracas which had arisen over the nude statues – and the 11-feet high figure, illuminated from within, showed the complete workings of the respiratory and digestive organs and the principle of the circulation of the blood.

This was all very well, complained David Graham in a letter to the *Evening Times* but "There are far too many ingenious wonders of mechanisation and not enough real life...The Concert Hall programme should be completely revised, for example the introduction of Continental bands would help. People will doubtless argue 'This is an Empire Exhibition' Perhaps it is, but music is universal."

Every day the newspapers in their Exhibition Dairies carried details of those men and women who made news and who would be visiting the Exhibition grounds. Briefly Australia was upsides with Canada when the attraction of the Mounties was offset by the visit of the champion sheep-shearer Don Munday. From South Africa came a party of bowlers, men and women, who were then touring Great Britain.

THE EMPIRE EXHIBITION OF 1938

From the United States came the noted broadcaster Ed Murrow who would earn a reputation as one of the world's leading combat zone reporters in the Second World War. Murrow broadcast across the Atlantic from the top of the Tower. New York was about to host the World's Fair in 1939 so there were many visitors from that city with an eye to picking up any good ideas and perhaps improving on them. Among these visitors was George McAneny, the chairman of directors. He was impressed by the Victoria Falls exhibit and the two thrusting young South Africans, Mormali Yule and Roderick Sechel, were commissioned to bring a model two-and-a-half times the size of the Bellahouston version to New York the following year. It would then be transported to Italy and form part of the Universal Exposition in Rome which was scheduled for 1942 and destined never to take place.

The Italian responsible for trade liaison, a Duke, was persuaded by that most famous of Glasgow journalists, Jack House, to take part in a broadcast from the BBC's new Glasgow studios in Queen Margaret Drive. He was collected from the Central Hotel by Jack House in a BBC limousine and as they were driving towards the studios, House, on consulting the broadcasting schedules, realised that His Grace would be appearing after Alfredo and his Gypsy Orchestra and before some other performance which was equally inappropriate. Fearing a diplomatic incident, House was saved by the fact that as the car drew up to the main entrance of Broadcasting house a distinguished-looking man emerged wearing a dinner-jacket. He was in fact an actor taking a breather on a sticky summer evening but the Duke assumed that he was a Corporation dignitary, quite possibly the Director-General, and engaged him in happy and animated conversation. The actor had the wit to carry out the part until such time as Jack House re-emerged, having secured the use of another, separate, studio.

The Aga Khan, who was actively involved in the work of the League of Nations and of course the spiritual head of many millions of the Empire's citizens, paid a visit in early July and spoke to an overflowing meeting in the Concert Hall. He then indulged his other main interest, racing, by visiting the Irish Pavilion, where he gazed enraptured at the many photographs of thoroughbreds and admired the Gold Cup which he himself had presented for international jumping competition and which was presently held by the Irish Army Team. He was accompanied by Alice Masaryk, the daughter of Jan Masaryk, once President of Czechoslovakia, whose country had less than three months independent existence left to it.

ORDINARY AND DISTINGUISHED VISITORS

TEA AMID THE TREE TOPS. The man on the extreme left is Mr Tait, the designer of the Tower.

Anthony Eden, who by his resignation from the Government two years before appeared to have damaged his political career irretrievably, paid a visit but it was a very subdued affair. He made no speeches and was quite outshone on the day by Don Bradman and the visiting Australian cricketers.

Not all the visitors from Europe were statesmen whose decisions affected vitally the Continental situation. Civil war was raging in Spain and Glasgow, with its Red tradition, was strongly on the side of the Republican Government. A party of refugee Basque school-children were given a guided tour of the Exhibition but photographs of the bombing of Guernica, an act which had aroused widespread revulsion, were removed until after the children had departed.

The stars of stage, films and radio who attended in large numbers will be dealt with elsewhere. They were made much of and added to the heightened atmosphere of Bellahouston, but infinitely more important were the ordinary citizens of Britain who came to marvel, to learn, and to enjoy.

The stratosphere girl. Camille Mayer performed incredible feats of acrobatics at the top of a 200 ft pole.

The stratosphere girl in performance. A few months later she was reported killed in Germany.

CHAPTER NINE
THAT'S ENTERTAINMENT

THE organisers of the Exhibition might have well described their aims as being threefold: to instruct, to edify and to entertain. They were keenly aware that a stage would arise in any individual visit when after the Corporation carpets of 1911 and 1937 had been inspected in the pavilion of their Glasgow maker's, Templeton, when the sheet from Robert Burns' Excise Book for December 1794 had been respectfully surveyed and when the crates of ivory and teak exhibits in the Burma Pavilion had been gazed at in wonder, there would come a need for diversion.

To that end a modern Concert Hall had been built which could accommodate in excess of 1,500 people. It was a stylish, modern building whose acoustics would be widely praised by world-renowned musicians but, designed as it was as a temporary building and one built for a summer season, there had seemed no need to put any form of heating in it and this was to prove a grievous handicap in this dampest and most depressing of summers.

There had been a real attempt made to cater for every conceivable taste. Variety was still in its heyday and above all, the late 1930s was quintessentially the period of the big dance bands. Everyone knew them from their radio broadcasts and many had actually seen them on stage, for it was common practice for a band such as Lew Stone's to form the second half of variety shows up and down the country. Sometimes musicians from one band would strike out on their own and form another. Nat Gonella did this when he left Lew Stone to set up for himself with the New Georgians.

All these great bands came to Bellahouston and most of them broadcast from the grounds either in concerts or in the regular series, The Exhibition on Parade. Nothing is more evocative of the 1930s than the recollection of their names. The Concert Hall opened with a visit from Ambrose, whose band had two girl vocalists. One of these, Evelyn Dall, was already nationally famous and the second youngster, whose name was Vera Lynn, would shortly be even more so. Yet the opening performances by the bands failed to attract people in numbers. It had nothing to do with the calibre of performance – the noted Scots character comedian, Will Fyffe, failed to draw an audience either and no Scots artiste was more popular than he was, except possibly Sir Harry Lauder who by then had virtually retired. It was simply that ticket prices which started at 2/6d and rose to a top price of 10/6d were felt to be seriously over-inflated. To listen to a symphony concert in Glasgow's excellent St Andrew's Halls would not involve more than a maximum expenditure of 7/6d – and St Andrew's Halls were heated! Redgauntlet had the right of it when he wrote in the *Evening Times:* "No concert hall in Glasgow at the height of winter season could hope to sustain continual interest night after night for six months so why should the Exhibition authorities imagine that they can do so in summer time and with such counter-attractions as Bellahouston offers right on their doorstep?"

As the Exhibition progressed and concert hall prices were cut, the audiences picked up. Ambrose was succeeded by the gentlemanly and reticent Henry Hall whose jerky delivery – "Good evening, ladies and gentlemen, this IS Henry Hall speaking" – had been for several years an invariable accompaniment of the broadcasts which his band made from Gleneagles Hotel, which was then owned by the London Midland and Scottish Railway. Other famous dance orchestras to appear were those of Harry Roy and Roy Fox. The visit of the latter's band caused especially keen interest, for a few months before a Glasgow girl, Mary Lee, born in Kinning Park, almost literally within sight of the Exhibition, had been plucked from obscurity to become one of the band's crooners. By the standards of the 1930s, this was celebrity indeed.

Big bands were literally household names and each had its signature. For Ambrose it was *When Day is Done*, the fast-rising Geraldo had *Hello Again!* for his broadcasts while Henry Hall had as his signing-off tune *Here's to the Next Time*. There were also those orchestras which favoured a particular kind of music or instrument. Among those engaged during the run of the Exhibition were Troise

THAT'S ENTERTAINMENT

Generals Haveloch and Outram greet each other at the Relief of the Siege of Lucknow. A scene from the Pageant of Scottish History which was written for the Exhibition.

and his Mandoliers, Alfredo and his Gypsy Orchestra and the then little-known Mantovani and his Tipica Orchestra. There was a resident Exhibition Band led by Billy Mason which although popular inevitably suffered somewhat from the more glamorous visitations already described. The band which really stopped the traffic was that of Jack Hylton, who came in the early autumn, by which time open-air dancing had become one of the most successful features of the entertainment side of the "Empirex". There was an attempt made to popularise a special dance written exclusively for Bellahouston, the Exhibition Swing, swing music being all the rage in 1938, but it failed to make any inroads on the Lambeth Walk, impregnably established. This was the title song of the show which starred Lupino Lane and Teddy St Dennis and each session of open-air dancing brought repeated demands that it should be played. Jack House, when the musical had looked like faltering in Glasgow, had persuaded its two stars to broadcast a couple of songs from BBC Glasgow which they cheerfully did without fee and after that the show never looked back.

To be candid, there were few lasting showbusiness successes of local dimension which arose from the Exhibition. The popular North-Eastern comedian Harry Gordon wrote a song called *Doon Bellahouston Way* but it had the short-lived vogue reserved for pantomine songs. The Scottish film-writer and playwright, Roger McDougall, later to achieve West End fame with his play, *To Dorothy a Son*, had rather more success with his attempt to introduce a new garment, the Bellahouston. He was then engaged in writing the scenario for the Hitchcock film *This Man is News* and with a Scottish colleague he took to appearing on set in a reversible jacket which was made of all-wool tartan on one side and rainproof poplin in the other. It is possible that only the outbreak of war prevented this ingenious jacket from achieving a wider production and success.

The lovers of classical music were well catered for and the quality of the artists engaged certainly matched the international importance of the occasion. Here again the story was of an admirable recovery after a bad, indeed embarrassing start. Discontent with the prices being charged had resulted in the BBC Scottish Symphony Orchestra playing to a chilled 50 people in the vast Concert Hall. Some of the artists engaged were swamped by the size of the hall – even the world-famous Glasgow Orpheus Choir under its conductor Hugh Roberton seemed somewhat uncomfortable. It was not an ideal venue for solo artists although Scotland's most gifted concert pianist, Frederic Lamond, certainly deserved more than the 200 hardy souls who turned out to hear his recital. The celebrated tenor from the Vienna State Opera, Alfred Piccaver was a better draw, perhaps proving the oft-repeated theory that to have a foreign name was a condition precedent of a successful musical career in pre-war Britain. He was accompanied by a young man who would become possibly the world's greatest accompanist, Gerald Moore.

There were disasters, notably those in which the Scottish Players gave performances of turgid Scottish dramas before a handful of relatives and friends and there was a Pageant Play about the Scots in Empire wherein the prologue was spoken

THAT'S ENTERTAINMENT

The lines of the bandstand are modern but the music played would have been familiar to those attending the Kelvingrove Exhibition of 1911, or indeed 1901.

by Maud Risdon and the conception was on as dire a level as such pageants invariably are.

But the great orchestras did well. The London Symphony Orchestra played for two nights under Sir Henry Wood, whose name was then synonymous with the Promenade Concerts, and Sir Adrian Boult conducted the BBC Symphony Orchestra. Most lavish in his praise was the ebullient Sir Thomas Beecham, who brought the London Philharmonic Orchestra to Glasgow and wrote the following in the Visitor's Book in the Concert Hall: "It is a splendid hall for music, clear and not over-resonant. When the Exhibition is over, it should be taken down and re-erected in some quarter of the city as a building for good concerts at cheap prices for a larger public." Given the melancholy fate of Glasgow concert halls in the almost-immediate future, this would have been a most timely suggestion, but like the advice of Queen Mary with regard to the refurbishing of tenement houses, it was not acted upon.

There was no difficulty in attracting a capacity audience where the performer was of truly international reputation. The marvellous American bass, Paul

THE EMPIRE EXHIBITION OF 1938

Midget Town, one of the more bizarre attractions of the Amusement Park.

Robeson, filled the Concert Hall not once but twice. After his first appearance in May he sent off his fee to the Spanish Civil War Relief Fund. He was universally known because of his records and his film appearances and for a sweetness of tone which was not common in singers of his range. By the time he returned in early September his concert had been sold out for days beforehand – people had queued for four hours to gain admission and £1 was being offered for the dearest tickets, those at 7/6d. Robeson greatly endeared himself to the Scottish audience when on the following morning, conscious that many thousands had been greatly disappointed in being unable to see and hear him, he paid an unexpected visit to The

THAT'S ENTERTAINMENT

Boys from the Queen Victoria School, Dunblane rehearsing for the Parade of the Boy Soldiers in the Exhibition Military Tattoo at Ibrox Park.

Clachan and to a delighted and surprised audience sang the *Eriskay Love Lilt* and *The Road to the Isles*. Paul Robeson claimed to have a working knowledge of Gaelic. He explained that he insisted on having at least a rudimentary knowledge of any language in which he was called upon to sing, so that he could interpret the feeling of the song more completely. Jack House recalls interviewing him at this time and asking him about his impressions of Scotland and the Scots to receive the unlooked-for reply, "They don't read their Bible enough", which would assuredly not have been how most Scots perceived themselves.

The outstanding success of Paul Robeson's impromptu recital at The Clachan points perhaps to a chance missed. The fanciful Highland village was enormously popular but depended entirely on its scenery, even to the extent of an elaborate backdrop of a loch which gave the impression of distance. It may well of course have been its tranquility which was the attraction but significantly when the Americans expressed interest in taking a similar exhibit to the New York World's Fair of 1939 they stipulated that there would have to be continuous exhibitions of piping, Highland dancing and Highland Games.

THE EMPIRE EXHIBITION OF 1938

Brigadoon would have to awaken considerably more often than once in a hundred years!

Another international musician who saw the "House Full" notices go up was the Viennese master violinist Fritz Kreisler. He was eminently well-equipped to give popular musical concerts because of his odd sense of humour. This consisted in "finding" forgotten or unknown works by such composers as Paganini and "re-introducing" them to grateful audiences and musicologists. Only much later, and sometimes never in his life time, would he reveal, or allow it to be discovered, that these charming lightweight pieces were his own compositions.

In the six months duration of the Exhibition a surprising number of film stars, British and American, made their way to Bellahouston. Gracie Fields, then at the height of her popularity and the epitome of British pluck in such films as *Sing as We Go*, spent a day at the Exhibition and attracted a crowd of 10,000 to the South bandstand where she sent them away happy after singing for them *Sally*, her signature tune, and *Little Old Lady*. It was revealed to her delighted fans that, however improbably, she was to play a Glasgow pub-owner in her next film *Shipyard Sally* which had as its theme the restart of work in the Clyde shipyards.

From Hollywood came Charles Laughton, British by birth and now American by choice, accompanied by his wife Elsa Lanchester. His recent performances as Henry VIII and as Captain Bligh in the film *Mutiny on the Bounty* had set new standards in film acting and he too was followed by large crowds wherever he went. He had come to promote his new film, *Vessel of Wrath* and in the midst of a seething crush of fans, told them rather ungallantly that he would rather be eating toffee apples and seeing round the exhibits. Lesser lights also had their day: the invaluable support actor Edward Everett Horton and the cowboy hero, Tom Mix, accompanied by his faithful horse, made their appearances.

Anna Neagle was especially welcome since her real name was Marjorie Robertson and since she had partly been brought up in the Mount Florida area of Glasgow. She had the unusual distinction of holding Season Ticket Number Two for the Exhibition – the coveted Number One was in the possession of a retired minister from the West End of the city. Her visit was felt to be doubly appropriate in view of the strong royal connection with the Exhibition since at that time, under the direction of her husband Herbert Wilcox, she had made a speciality of playing Queen Victoria in such films as *Victoria Regina* and *Sixty Glorious*

THAT'S ENTERTAINMENT

The 4th/7th Dragoons rehearse for the Musical Ride.

Years. The Scottish première of the latter film was in fact shown at the Empire Exhibition.

Most poignant of all the visits made by the film stars was that of Eddie Cantor. He had toured the Exhibition in the morning and had caused considerable offence, although certainly unwittingly, by being photographed sitting on the head of one of the lions outside the Scottish Pavilion. He did not stay for lunch but returned to the centre of the city where the underlying purpose of his visit became apparent. Speaking to a Jewish charitable organisation, the B'nai Brith, in the Ca'doro Restaurant he gave them a chilling message. He stated that to his certain knowledge it was now too late to do anything for the adult Jews in a Europe which was increasingly coming under Nazi domination but that some children at least might be saved if enough money to bribe the officials concerned could be raised. "You

THE EMPIRE EXHIBITION OF 1938

can't even try to save the poor parents. They're beyond that, but the children must be given a chance to live."

For a full hour Cantor hectored his audience mercilessly. "I never heard of anyone having a breakdown because of work done for charity nor have I heard of a man who went bankrupt because of what he gave for charity. If you deserve the name of Jews then take these children out of Germany and Austria." He asked for, and got, £10,000. With an almost unbelievable resilience of spirit he then returned to Bellahouston and charmed the crowds with performances of his best-known songs *If You Knew Suzy* and *Makin' Whoopee*. His broadcast, too, was highly successful.

In the fearful weeks of Munich the Exhibition entertainments did much to reassure people and divert them. Identifiable mistakes were made, though, and some visitors made little impact – the days of such as the veteran Music Hall performer Florrie Forde were regrettably but inevitably past. It was never likely that the novelty pianist Billy Mayerl or the variety act Flotsam and Jetsam – the Flanders and Swann of their day – would come anywhere near filling the Concert Hall and the String Quartets were literally misplaced. With the only absolutely exact science known to man, hindsight, certain things would have been done differently. The Concert Hall would have been heated. It would have been free to all except for the genuine celebrity concerts. There would have been more wet-weather entertainment and some of the bands, rather than dance orchestras, could have been allowed to perform in larger buildings. There was a case to be made for having provided trios or quartets in the cafés and perhaps some vaudeville acts.

But this was the wisdom of the morning after. The crowds who thronged the various drives and avenues of the Exhibition had been intrigued by the news that the famous woman flyer, Amy Mollison, was taking part in the Empirex Motor Rally which was an offshoot of the Exhibition. They had been able to witness the large-scale parade of the animals and performers of Bertram Mills' Circus, then appearing at Cathkin Park in the Crosshill district of Glasgow, who had eagerly seized the opportunity of such a marvellous display cabinet. As they, the spectators, packed their increasingly tired and fractious children on to the Corporation tram-cars which would convey them to distant parts of the city they could reflect that for six months Glasgow had in truth been one of the entertainment capitals of the world.

THAT'S ENTERTAINMENT

The daily mannequin parades in the Fashion Theatre could always guarantee a crowd.

And, in the best traditions of industrial Exhibitions there was a spin-off for the film industry in Scotland. The Empire Cinema, theoretically under the direction of A. B. King (later Sir Alexander King) but for day-to-day purposes controlled by Charles Oakley, Henry Watt and John Grierson, put on daily programmes of the kind familiar to those who patronised news cinemas. These programmes lasted for about one hour and might typically contain a newsreel, a cartoon, a travelogue and two documentaries, one British and one from the Empire.

The 1930s was the great age of the documentary film, Robert Flaherty had made *Drifters* and *Man of Aran* and the Post Office Film Unit had recruited the talents of W. H. Auden and Benjamin Britten to make *Night Mail*. John Grierson, a brusque dour Scot, was inspired to follow them, heartened by the fact that the noted film director, Alfred Hitchcock, had come north to act as adjudicator for the British Empire Amateur Film Festival. The Films of Scotland Committee, founded by Grierson with the avowed intention of supplying documentary films about Scotland, was one of the longest-lived legacies of the Exhibition, carrying on until 1982, and had the great distinction of winning a Hollywood Oscar with *Seaward the Great Ships*. Before that it had made an impact in 1938 with such gritty documentaries as *Sea Food* and *The North Sea* which took an unsentimental look at the Scottish fishing industry.

The Exhibition had allowed Scottish artists to display their talents to a wider audience than would normally have been available to them and, just as importantly, had given them standards of excellence to which to aspire. For that, if for nothing else, it would have been worthwhile.

CHAPTER TEN
HOW THE FUTURE MIGHT HAVE LOOKED

ONE of the abiding fascinations of the Empire Exhibition of 1938 lies in its architecture, the flat roofs, the ship's bridge frontages, the juxtaposition of the curve and the straight line. Seen from the air, it conveyed the impression of a film set for *The War of the Worlds* or *Things To Come*. In the event, it was the architecture which was never built. It was the way Scotland might well have looked had the Forties been a peaceful decade. As it was all non-essential construction had come to a halt within months of the last night at Bellahouston and by the time peace had been restored and the need for building licences removed – and the austerity of the ten post-war years had been every bit as rigorous as the war itself – 15 years had elapsed and ideas in design had altered. A few roadhouses, one or two government buildings, a handful of hotels, schools and the scattered relics of the once numerous cinemas of the period are all that remain of what might have been an alternative way.

It was an enormous pity that the publicists of the Exhibition did not take full advantage of the good press which the lay-out of the site received from the opinion-forming newspapers in England. There was never much commercial enthusiasm for the venture in the south but the organising committee could certainly not have complained of this "notice" in *The Times* two days after the Exhibition opened: "A year or so ago, while the Glasgow Exhibition was in embryo, many must have felt fears of a junior Wembley. But it is clear that Bellahouston has a beauty and vitality such as Wembley with its well-meaning stolidity never possessed. Lord Elgin and his colleagues and advisers – with Mr Thomas Tait architect-in-chief – have created not another Wembley but something at once more dignified and less solemn."

THE EMPIRE EXHIBITION OF 1938

A reader's letter to *The Observer* on 8 May 1938 made the same point though more obliquely and at the expense of Wembley: "It had the largest and heaviest of buildings since the Pyramids. It had not the advantage of learning from the Paris Exhibition of 1937 how to be gay and brilliant and yet incomparably progressive. And then let us admit that it was not so much an Empire Exhibition as the Empire making an exhibition of itself. Not so the superb success at Bellahouston."

All this was very flattering, and more academic approval was not lacking either. In an article in the *Manchester Guardian*, C. H. Reilly, Emeritus Professor of Architecture at the University of Liverpool, spoke highly of the "energy" of the buildings he had seen in Glasgow: "Not since the great Exhibition of 1851, the parent of all such things, has an exhibition in this country shown such unity of style in its building as the present one in Glasgow. What is important too and it is a thing that could not have happened any time in the past 150 years till today, the style of the buildings is not an assumed or a reproduced one but a vital and living one growing naturally out of the chief material used – that is to say steel in its various forms."

Professor Reilly then went on to praise the use of coloured frescoes throughout the Exhibition: "The storms and rains of the last few weeks don't seem to have affected them. If, as seems likely, some permanent method has been found of painting large-scale decoration on exterior plaster surfaces, and if in future we mean to keep our towns clean, then it seems likely with the concentrated windows of modern buildings, leaving great plain surfaces everywhere, we may shortly be seeing such decorations in the streets of our towns to their great enlivenment and interest and to the destruction of other and more crude forms of advertisement."

In every sense of the word, the Tower of Empire dominated the Exhibition although it was much more commonly referred to as Tait's Tower. It was the responsibility of Thomas S. Tait who was determined to exercise a literal and metaphorical overall view of the Exhibition. He was determined that there should be a unifying hand, that the detritus of the Exhibition, the street furniture as it were, should not be allowed to detract from the carefully thought out overall scheme.

The construction of the Colonial and Dominions pavilions was in their own hands. Tait encouraged private companies to enlist architects such as Basil Spence, who was responsible for the ICI Pavilion. Alister MacDonald, son of the Prime Minister, Ramsay MacDonald, was in charge of the Peace Pavilion, perhaps more prestigious than it sounds because there were still many people even in 1938 who

HOW THE FUTURE MIGHT HAVE LOOKED

The Church of Scotland Pavilion, a tryst for overseas visitors.

felt that the League of Nations might still manage to avert the threatened European war. MacDonald had also been the designer of the Empire Theatre which showed the Exhibition films. Young Scottish architects such as Jack Coia were given their chance on the Palace of Industry and it was pleasing to note that a woman, Margaret Brodie, had been entrusted with the Women of the Empire Pavilion.

In his excellent book *The Scottish Thirties – An Architectural Introduction*, Charles McKean has this revealing quote from Tait: "Scotland to my mind had probably the most instinctive feeling for colour . . . I made every effort to prevent any feeling of drabness, solemnity or sadness . . . even in northern industrial

THE EMPIRE EXHIBITION OF 1938

towns it is possible by judicious use of colour to achieve a spirit of happiness – and life."

In no other imaginable sector could Tait have been more of a benefactor to the working people who flocked to Bellahouston to see buildings in unheard-of pinks, reds, blues and creams. Coming from an environment of soot-encrusted stone tenements, where the original grey stone had long since blackened evilly, their lives were permeated by drabness. This was reflected in their dress and for much of the winter they groped their way through sulphurous industrial fog. Even during the months of the Exhibition there were days on which the view from the top of the Tower was minimal, shut out by the pall of factory smoke which hung heavily on the city. Those who believed in the essential villainy of the private landlord (and there were many such on the Labour benches of Glasgow Corporation) were transported with joy when the National Federation of Property Owners objected to the depiction of a slum kitchen only to be informed that the exhibit was part of an actual property.

The Tower of Empire which a Danish architect was to describe as "daemonically vertical" had been badly served by the original artist's impression and it was ably defended by Captain Salvesen, the vice-chairman of the Executive Committee when addressing Falkirk Rotary Club: "The public plans of the proposed Tower make it look like an aeroplane which has nose-dived on a hill but I am confident that when the Tower is erected it will prove a noble feature of the Empire Exhibition. Indeed I would hope that it may become a permanent feature of the park."

The sheer statistics of the edifice were of themselves sufficiently imposing. It weighed 3,200 tons and concrete to a depth of 21 feet six inches had been poured into a cavity excavated in the knoll. By a real stroke of fortune the soil was pure boulder clay which made the work of securing a foundation infinitely easier and cheaper. Colville's of Motherwell provided the high tensile ducol steel for the angles twelve inches by twelve inches by seven-eighths of an inch.

One of the best pieces of writing about the Tower is contained in the leaflet of 1937, *Scotland Calling*, in the section headed "From the Top of the Tower". It merits reproduction in full:

"A tower that will rise from the crest of the hill in one unbroken sweep of 300 feet, an all-metal skyscraper, streamlined and pencil-thin. A specialist's job. The

HOW THE FUTURE MIGHT HAVE LOOKED

KEEP YOUNG and BEAUTIFUL. *The Women's League of Health and Beauty was in its hey day in the 1930s.*

planning of its steelwork is beyond the range of everyday engineering for no tower of its height and design has yet been built to withstand the strain it will be called upon to carry. Yet six hundred people will be able to stand in safety on its observation platforms and see spread out below them the British Empire in miniature.

"Thomas S. Tait, FRIBA, architect of the Exhibition and of Sydney Harbour Bridge designed it. Scotland already calls it 'Tait's Tower'.

"The trees round its base thin out and disappear as the ground drops to the level parkland below the hill. There are 170 acres of that parkland. Last year they were just a park. Next year they will be the home of the greatest Empire Exhibition the world has known for fourteen years, a playground and a market-place conceived in the grand manner.

"On this park and on the hill rising from its centre are taking shape the palaces and pavilions which next year will make Glasgow the unofficial capital of the Empire. From the top of the Tower the Exhibition will be spread out like a map. The people swarming along its avenues will appear small, dwarfed not only by distance but by the buildings round them. Where sober citizens played golf a few short months ago will be a lake, floodlit at night and sprayed by fountains by day. Yonder lie the pavilions of Canada, Australia, New Zealand and South Africa. On the fringe of the hill are the Colonies.

From the base of the Tower will flow cascades of floodlit water. Down both sides of the hill they will flow, each flanked by wide stairways, through a series of lily-pools to the palaces on the low ground, leading the eye from the industrial section and the amusement park to the Scottish Pavilions, the British Government Pavilions, the Palace of Arts and the Concert Hall. Banks of flowers will line the avenues, harmonising with the gay colours of the pavilions which are themselves only part of the great colour scheme covering the whole Exhibition.

"And there are trees – on the hill, along the avenues, among the pavilions and Kiosks – trees carefully preserved so that they might play their part in making the Exhibition beautiful as well as gay. Bellahouston Park is well wooded: the whole Exhibition has been planned to take advantage of its trees. When darkness falls and the floodlights are switched on, their leaves and branches will be one of the most striking pictures the Exhibition has to offer.

"But that is only the foreground. The Exhibition presents the Empire in minature; the Tower presents Scotland in detail, from the Highlands of the North to the Southern Lowlands. The bens and glens cut the horizon. The lochs of the Highlands catch and reflect the sunshine. And between the Exhibition and the mountains flows the Clyde, with the clang and clatter of its famous shipyards carrying across the roof-tops to the Tower."

Care for the environment was a feature of the great jamboree of 1938. The Treetops restaurant had been built with a specially designed roof to avoid having to lop or cut down any of the trees in the park. It is interesting to note that on the next great occasion in the park's history, more than 40 years later when Pope

HOW THE FUTURE MIGHT HAVE LOOKED

The scale models of ocean-going liners, in this case the Mauretiania, *were a particular attraction of the Palace of Engineering.*

John Paul II said Mass there on his visit to Scotland, the Bellahouston trees were once more at the centre of a controversy.

The scale and complexity of the fountains astonished all those who saw them. They were especially impressive after dark as the waters changed colour and appeared to dance. Nothing on that scale had been attempted before or has been since and most fortunately an amateur film enthusiast shot them in colour so that a record of them exists in the vaults of the Scottish Film Archives.

As the Exhibition drew to a close the question arose as to what should be done with the buildings which C.H. Reilly, Emeritus Professor of Architecture at the

THE EMPIRE EXHIBITION OF 1938

THE STRIKING CATHOLIC PAVILION. *The work of Jack Coia.*

University of Liverpool, had described as "crude but invigorating". In late July Glasgow Corporation was asked what buildings it might wish to retain. The Palace of Arts was a permanent structure and would remain anyway and this was also the intention for the Tower. It was suggested that the Corporation might also wish to retain the Palace of Engineering and the Concert Hall. When the offer was declined the elected body came in for severe criticism but in all fairness the matter was more complicated than a straightforward acceptance or rejection. Retaining

HOW THE FUTURE MIGHT HAVE LOOKED

The Clachan and "sea loch" beyond!

the Concert Hall meant installing an expensive heating system and/or re-locating the structure. No commercial manager would have been sanguine enough to think that he would make a profit in a hall out at Bellahouston in winter once the surrounding attractions had been removed. The Corporation too was bound to restore the park to its previous usage on behalf of the ratepayers.

There had been a move to keep the Exhibition open during the summer of 1939 but it was wisely decided not to pursue this possibility. There would inevitably have been a sense of anti-climax and the attention of the world of exhibitions would have shifted to New York where the World's Fair was due to be held. Sir Cecil Weir (he had been knighted in the Birthday Honours List) argued for the retention of a portion of it to hold a display of British industry, but there was little enthusiasm for his suggestion. Thomas S. Tait was one of his few supporters. He maintained

THE EMPIRE EXHIBITION OF 1938

"Have a shot, did you say? No' me, I get a' the shooglin' I want in the Corporation 'buses."

that the buildings, although almost exclusively temporary, could easily stand for another year.

Mr Ernest Brown MP, the Minister of Labour strongly asserted that the Tower should be maintained as a permanent monument but even this did not eventuate. Various conflicting reasons were put forward. The Tower would be a hazard for aircraft approaching the city airport which was then located rather nearer to the city centre at Renfrew. Another variation on the same theme was that in the event of war the Tower would furnish too good a guide and marker for enemy aircraft although the logic of that argument would have led to the dismantling of the tower of Glasgow University which stood on an equally visible hill slope on the opposite bank of the Clyde.

Even the retention of the lakes and floral gardens, for which future Lord Provost

HOW THE FUTURE MIGHT HAVE LOOKED

To-Day's Hero

The man who asked for a pie and chips at the Atlantic Restaurant.

The Atlantic was the most exclusive and most expensive of the Exhibition restaurants.

Patrick Dollan pleaded with great eloquence, was not found possible. There was a sense of waste, of an opportunity thrown away, and Walter Elliott, Minister of Health, expressed this though his last few words had a most unministerial humility. Speaking on 21 October he said, "It seems a pity to attempt in ten days' time to sweep the whole thing away and reduce it again to a park and a golf course but who am I to dogmatise about it?" With a Philistine practicality the Corporation Art Galleries and Museums Committee which made the final Palace of Arts inspection bought only the office furniture for the city.

The upshot was that the work of dismantling the Exhibition began before the last spectator had fairly left the grounds. An army of workmen dismantled, unscrewed, carried away. The last stand of Treasurer Dollan – that the Palace of Engineering could be adapted to seat 20,000 people and that the citizens ought to be asked by plebiscite which buildings they wished to retain – was as unavailing as last stands usually are. It was his opinion that the Corporation should purchase the Exhibition lock, stock and barrel but perhaps financial canniness prevailed, or more likely, since civic thrift was a comparative rarity, there was the realisation that the park might be required for grimmer purposes before long and indeed it was. Within two years the site of the Exhibition was at various times a transit camp for French troops evacuated from the disastrous Norwegian campaign, in another two it was a receiving station for prisoners-of-war, mostly, but not exclusively, Italian. From time to time British soldiers were quartered there too, but in the main, and even in wartime conditions, the park was returned to the use of the citizens of Glasgow as the majority of the members of the Corporation of that city had wished it to be.

In the end therefore it worked out as planned. Starting at midnight on 29 October 1938 the exhibitors removed at their own cost exhibits, stands, fittings and anything else pertaining to their display. All exhibition spaces and ground sites were cleared by the end of November and by the beginning of 1939 all ground sites had been cleared and made good.

The Palace of Engineering went off to Prestwick, the South African Pavilion also ended up in Ayrshire, having been offered to and rejected by Glasgow, where in a much modified form it served as a guest-house for Imperial Chemicals Limited. The Empire Cinema may or may not have been transported to Lochgilphead. The visitor to Bellahouston Park today can see the Palace of Arts as it was. For the rest he or she must rely on photographic reconstruction and a powerful imagination.

A handful of hotels and roadhouses, the occasional school and hospital, a last fugitive cinema, these are practically all that is left to remind us what the 1940s might have looked like. In an editorial on the day after the Exhibition closed, the *Glasgow Herald* pointed to a chance that would be missed, although the writer did not know that: "It would be difficult to over-estimate the part played by Mr T.S. Tait, the architect of the Exhibition for his imagination in adopting an admittedly favourable site to a design that was at once simple, direct and conceived in the modern idiom. Even on days of rain when the rest of Glasgow was grey and

HOW THE FUTURE MIGHT HAVE LOOKED

The Atlantic Restaurant.

depressing, Bellahouston still continued to remain gay and fresh. The lesson will not be lost on Scotland that form and colour in architecture can be very effective antidotes to the worst features of the climate.

DRENCHED and UNHAPPY. *Coachmen of the Lord Mayor of London.*

CHAPTER ELEVEN
SEPTEMBER (AND OCTOBER) IN THE RAIN

THERE was a marvellous aptness in the words of one of the popular songs of 1938 which in a way was to become the theme song of the latter weeks of the Exhibition:

The leaves of brown came tumbling down,
Remember,
That September,
In the rain.

As one sodden, gusty week succeeded another, it was hard to recall that drought had seemed the one great problem back in April when indeed there had been only two brief showers between 6 April and the middle of May. At least that prolonged dry spell had been crucial to the Exhibition's opening on time. Work had proceeded almost unhindered from January to May, allowing among other things the 20 miles or more of underground electric cable to be laid. Now, however, the wretched weather was seriously affecting attendances, with the additional worry that the very worst excesses of the climate seemed to reserve themselves invariably for the weekends when the largest attendances would normally have been expected.

The organising committee reacted to these crises with imagination and promptitude. At the end of July it had been decided to issue monthly and three-monthly season tickets. There had already been a precedent for this with the issue of weekly season tickets during the period of the Glasgow Fair holidays. From time to time

THE EMPIRE EXHIBITION OF 1938

people had complained about Exhibition prices but the price of the full-term season ticket (to run for six months) had been most reasonable. Adults were charged 25 shillings and children 10/6d, sums which compared very well with the guinea and half-guinea which had been required for the Exhibition of 1901. With tongue in cheek Jack House claims that the great moment of the Exhibition of 1938 for him was when he realised very early on that he had already had his money's worth and from now on all his entertainment was free.

On the last Saturday of July the weather was so abominable that only 71,000 people attended when well over 200,000 were expected. The question of Sunday opening was canvassed yet again, with an equally negative response. As a mark of the diminution in the numbers attending, 28 turnstile attendants found themselves prematurely dismissed. An awesome electrical storm on 11 August caused some structural damage and severe flooding to the depth of one foot of water.

Royal visits could retrieve the situation in part at least. When Queen Mary made the most publicised of her several visits on Saturday, 10 September, she attracted a crowd of 235,209, a record for any single day during the Exhibition's run. The weather, however, remained grim, unrelenting. On 14 October a gale which reached 70 miles per hour caused two huge glass windows in the western side of the Treetops Restaurant to cave in, causing heavy damage.

During the six months the Exhibition was operating the rainfall for the Glasgow district was recorded as 23.75 inches as against a normal 18.49 for the months in question. June and October were particularly bad although August was pretty dry. Oddly, the sunshine figure was also good, with 831.5 hours of sunshine as against the 811.4, which was normal, but all too often the sunshine occurred before the Exhibition got under way or late in the day when people had decided not to risk it.

The other factor which was greatly perturbing the backers of the Empire Exhibition was the deteriorating international situation. Throughout August and September Europe seemed to be heading irreversibly towards its second world war in 20 years. It was literally true that there were men attending the Exhibition who had fought in France in 1918 and were still less than 40 years of age. Hitler had taken over Austria in the Anschluss of March 1938 and throughout the summer had been making bellicose utterances on the subject of Czechoslovakia. By the end of August, despite Chamberlain's protestations that this was a faraway country of which we knew little or nothing, it did seem likely that Britain would be forced

SEPTEMBER (AND OCTOBER) IN THE RAIN

The brilliant floodlights of the Exhibition (of a scale never before seen in Scotland) ominously illuminate the aircraft carrier on the front of the Palace of Engineering. In marked contrast Scots would spend the next six years in almost total darkness.

shamefacedly into war as the appeals of President Benes and the young Masaryk from Prague grew more heart-rending. The special Exhibition editions of the newspapers began to carry headlines featuring previously unfamiliar geographical and proper names. Henlein, the leader of the Germans in the Sudetenland, was protesting every day against atrocities, real or alleged, committed against the minority German population by Czech policemen and soldiers.

Attendances at Bellahouston fell off as people with a sick horror remembered the carnage of the First World War. Glasgow, which had volunteered its men for the Colours with great enthusiasm, had suffered perceptibly more heavily than the great English industrial cities such as Birmingham and Newcastle. This trend had been accentuated by the prestige of the Scottish regiments and the fact that recruiting had been done on not only a territorial but also on an occupational basis.

THE EMPIRE EXHIBITION OF 1938

The railwaymen, the Stock Exchange clerks, had suffered fearful losses, and the Scottish bantam battalions (the minimum height for recruitment to Scottish regiments was an astonishing five feet two inches) had been cut down in swathes.

Reservists now waited with every post for a recall to the Colours, air raid precautions were introduced with simulated attacks and trenches were dug in the parks, including Bellahouston, although beyond the lines of the Exhibition itself. Queues began to form at the Army and Navy Pavilion and at the same site women began enrolling in the Auxiliary Territorial Service as the women's organisation which was to be the forerunner of the Women's Royal Army Corps was then called.

It is interesting that neither Jack House nor Charles Oakley remembers any great degree of recruiting fervour even in the last days of the Exhibition but inevitably thoughts turned to the possibility of war. The armed forces put some of their most modern equipment on display, a four-ton light tank, a 14-ton medium tank and a six-ton armoured car were all demonstrated to those who in the very near future would be called upon to use them. Tradition was not neglected, for also on view were the sword and scabbard of Ensign Ewart who at Waterloo had captured the Eagle of the 45th "Invincibles". From an earlier stage of the same war came a recruiting poster of 1794 for the Seaforth Highlanders. With the typical *élan* of the period it bore the injunction: "Now for a stroke at the Monsieurs m'boys! King George for ever! Hurrah!"

Suddenly, out of the blue, the Prime Minister, Neville Chamberlain, announced that he had been invited to meet the European leaders, Daladier of France, Hitler and Mussolini at Munich. For a week the country held its breath. It had already been decided that the international situation was so serious that the King would be unable to come north again for the launching of the *Queen Elizabeth*. That would have to be performed by the Queen herself, but the National Mod which was this year scheduled to be part of the Exhibition, went ahead.

At the very end of September the Prime Minister returned from Germany bearing details of the Munich Agreement and received a hero's welcome. Those who opposed the settlement and maintained that Czechoslovakia had been cast as sacrificial lamb received scant public sympathy at the time. The country had been terrified by the prospect of war but now had a year to come to the conclusion that in the long term war could not be avoided. When it came, in 1939, there was a profound feeling of calm, almost anti-climax.

SEPTEMBER (AND OCTOBER) IN THE RAIN

Neon lights and puddles. An all too familiar feature of the summer months.

It was widely believed that Mr Chamberlain himself would pay a visit to the Exhibition. The guarantors must devoutly have hoped for this for at that time he would have exceeded even Queen Mary in drawing-power, but it was not to be and his only direct connection with the Exhibition was in the manifesto which he had issued before its start. With wishful thinking it was even suggested that Benito Mussolini might be prevailed upon to pay a late visit. He then enjoyed a certain amount of popularity, being credited with helping to restrain Hitler at Munich.

At the beginning of October there was a Mafeking-like atmosphere and the crowds flocked back to the open-air dancing. They shuffled sedately around the pathways and avenues, occasionally breaking out into the incongruous Cockney strains of the hit song of the day:

> Any evening, any day,
> Take a walk down Lambeth way,
> You'll find them all,
> Doing the Lambeth Walk. Oi!

The few who were more perceptive knew better. It was decided to hold three mock air raids during the last week of the Exhibition and to carry through the large ARP exercises which had been originally planned. There would be a massive Civil Defence Exercise staged at Hampden Park in the following April.

Meanwhile attendances figures would be boosted by the decision to give free admission to 80,000 jobless in the last fortnight of the Exhibition season. The cost of this would be shared by the Corporation of Glasgow and the Exhibition authorities. That the Exhibition had been good for West of Scotland employment, even in the short term, was indirectly revealed by the fact that its close-down would mean that 7,000 jobs would go.

Towards the end of October the winding-down process began, although the Exhibition was to go out on the highest of notes. It was decided that the last night should be a gala night. There was a large Empirex Ball in St Andrew's Halls, as there had been at the start of things in May. The President, the Earl of Elgin, broadcast to the Empire and he and his Countess were presented with their portraits in oils. It was a deserved presentation. He had worked strenuously and well to make the Exhibition a success and Lady Elgin had been undeviating in her support.

The Exhibition would close its doors on Saturday, 29 October, and it was thought that as many as 300,000 might come on that day. It was to be a gala day. Sir Cecil M. Weir set the tone when he said in a statement: "Let the last day, Saturday October 29 be as memorable and unforgettable as those wonderful days when our beloved sovereigns, King George and Queen Elizabeth, our beloved Queen Mother and all members of the Royal Family by their personal presence among their devoted people in Bellahouston Park added lustre, renown and distinction to Scotland's great Empire Exhibition."

SEPTEMBER (AND OCTOBER) IN THE RAIN

Exhibition souvenirs, such as the one illustrated, were greatly in demand.

By the time the last day dawned, more than 12 million visitors and passed through the turnstiles. The formal closing ceremony was to take place at 3.15 p.m. but nobody would pay too much attention to that. What would happen in the last hour was far more important. At 11.15 p.m. four pipe bands would parade from the South Bandstand all around the grounds and it was hoped that many of those

THE EMPIRE EXHIBITION OF 1938

THE ICI PAVILION. *The work of Sir Basil Spence, this too had its admirers, many people believing that it was the most striking building of the entire Exhibition.*

present would follow them on their route. When they returned to the South Bandstand the vast assembly would join in the singing of *Auld Lang Syne* and the National Anthem and on the stroke of midnight the Union Jack would be struck from the Tower and the floodlights dim and die on the tall noble structure. "Watch the Tower" was the watchword given to those going along that last evening.

The last piece of entertainment was a macabre foretaste of what lay ahead. Three Hawker Hinds staged a mock attack on the Exhibition and were driven off by artillery and caught by searchlights manned by personnel from 603 City of Glasgow Squadron which was stationed at Abbotsinch. The problematic success of the eight guns and three searchlights had less to do with what was likely to have happened than with the need to reassure a jittery civilian population which a few short weeks before had stood in the very antechamber of war. Even so, there were those who remembered Guernica, Barcelona and Madrid...and wondered.

The weather was unrelentingly malign to the very last, the final three hours bringing a torrential downpour as had happened in 1901 and again in 1911. Yet a swarming horde of 364,092 people had made their way through the turnstiles, fought for souvenirs and trampled the grass to a black pulp. Five hundred Corporation tramcars had been deployed on the loop which surrounded the park to ferry the last-night crowds home, but despite the commendable efficiency of the service which they provided thousands of people were still roaming around the Mosspark district at four o'clock in the morning. Traffic jams were of heroic proportions and hundreds of cars were abandoned by their owners, to be retrieved on the calmer Sabbath. The Exhibition was over. It remained only for the jury to bring in the verdict.

The main entrance gate.

CHAPTER TWELVE
LOOK ON MY WORKS YE MIGHTY AND DESPAIR

IT would not be too difficult to make out a case that the Empire Exhibition had been less than an unqualified success. Throughout its run it had been hampered by dreadful weather and a troubled political situation. It had been inadequately advertised in England and scarcely at all in Canada and the United States. There had been times in the run-up to it when capital and labour each had eyed the other side with even more distrust than usual and pondered its motives. Alone among the four Glasgow exhibitions it had needed to call upon the guarantors to make good their promises. The loss was not inordinate – three shillings and fivepence in the pound was what the guarantors were required to find – but the hope had been that there would be a comfortable surplus which could be distributed among worthy and approved causes. The question, therefore, had to be asked: had all the preparation, all the work, all the effort been worthwhile at the end of the day?

The answer had to be a resounding yes. The unanimous recollection, half a century on, of those who attended the great event is of the tremendous joy and delight, the overpowering sense of wonder which they derived from what was on show at Bellahouston. Thousands of Scots had been introduced to soft ice-cream, to Tim the Speaking Clock, to the girl shoe-blacks, to the Dursley trucks, to the Boy Scouts and Rovers who had acted as guides to the VIP cars. It had brought Glasgow to centre-stage at a time when industry, political power and even major-ranking entertainment had seemed to be flowing from it.

Who had gained from the Exhibition? The two young men who ran the Victoria Falls exhibit certainly. Such was the attraction of their model that a broken drive belt which took five hours to repair cost them well over £200 in takings. The Irish

THE EMPIRE EXHIBITION OF 1938

Pavilion had done well with over 260,000 items of agricultural produce sold and the Australian Pavilion had been unable to keep pace with the demand for apples. The Post Office too had prospered with 10,000 postcards per day sent from the Exhibition Post Office, by far the bulk of them collected from the postbox in the Clachan which was easily the favourite view. The special postmark, 'Exhibition Glasgow', was greatly in demand by philatelists. The makers of souvenirs had seen them go briskly, the paper-knives, tea caddies, tea-strainers, handkerchiefs and aprons all bearing representations either of the Tower, the Clachan or the red lion which was the symbol of the Empire Exhibition of 1938.

The effect on the larger economy was more uncertain. The Clyde coast towns complained that on Bank Holidays Glaswegians were going to Bellahouston rather than Rothesay, Largs or Dunoon. There was an upturn in the number of overseas visitors coming to Scotland and for this the Exhibition was entitled to claim some credit. There had been however reduced takings for shopkeepers in Paisley, Greenock and other near neighbours of Bellahouston and they were unlikely to mourn too long or too deeply when the "big house" put up its shutters.

No one then knew that a unique privilege had been conferred upon the city in that it had been the site of the last Durbar, the last great assemblage of Empire. Never again could there be such a comprehensive review of the Empire at work and at play. Such comment as there was at the time could not know this. The *Glasgow Herald* was strangely subdued in its assessment in its leader article of 31 October 1938: "The impression remains that the hand of tradition lay rather heavily on the Exhibition. If there have been mild complaints that some of the pavilions have been little more than bazaars, that is a defect that appears inherent in exhibitions. Yet the sort of half-hearted support that was given by some of the Colonial Governments whose total contribution to the Exhibition was in some instances the contents of a small glass case scarcely postulates the kind of enthusiasm for an Empire enterprise that might have been expected in the circumstances. But better to have made only a microscopic contribution to this Empire in miniature than, as in the case of the Government of India, no contribution at all."

Behind the lines in the *Herald* is the implied criticism that Government Departments in the south had not used sufficient muscle to persuade people overseas to exhibit. It was felt that London had shown its usual interest in and support for

The tower illuminated.

things located in Scotland, almost none. This lackadaisical attitude was contrasted with the speedy demand for the return of the great Globe of Empire to the Board of Trade once the Exhibition closed.

Patrick Dollan, probably the most visionary of Scottish local politicians, got it more nearly right when after lamenting the decision not to hold a plebiscite on those buildings which should be retained for the citizens of Glasgow – "plebiscites have been held on many less important things" – he went on to say this: "I feel that the Exhibition has taught all of us a finer and more colourful way of living and that it is possible in Glasgow to educate and enjoy ourselves without drabness and greyness."

THE EMPIRE EXHIBITION OF 1938

In those words he articulated precisely what his fellow-citizens felt at the time and still felt 50 years on. They had had the satisfaction of seeing the astonishment of the English visitors at the level of sophistication on offer at Bellahouston. Nor would anyone else ever see again that which they had seen, for the British Empire was on the point of death.

The smiling Gurkhas, the courteous impeccable Mounties, the strange giraffe-necked women from Africa went home, vanished as if they were wisps of a cloudy, insubstantial, Imperial dream. The quick-following war, with French Canadians refusing to fight in the Empire's cause and South African troops being largely reserved for the African theatre of conflict, taught the perceptive that Britain might win or lose the titanic struggle on which she was now embarked but that Bellahouston had indeed been the last Durbar.

Did the politicians know this even as, with the Scottish industrialists and aristocracy, they had planned the Exhibition throughout the previous two years? Almost certainly not. Our imputations are made with hindsight. Who shall say whether the Empire was destroyed by the military forces of Germany and Italy or by the psychological cleverness of the Japanese in systematically humiliating and degrading captured British officers? We can see now that there was no way back from Singapore and Hong Kong, despite the fraudulent victory of 1945. Perhaps financial pressures and indebtedness to the United States finally undid us, for it was an error to think that all the opponents of the British Empire fought on the other side. Certainly British Imperial aspirations had few enemies more implacable or more determined than Franklin Delano Roosevelt.

Whatever the reason, the British Empire took and gave its benefit performance in Glasgow in the summer of 1938 to be replaced by a Commonwealth which would grow ever more amorphous with the passing of time. Those excellent barometers of a country's imperial health, children's papers, would reflect the change. No longer was it credible that one of the three houses at Red Circle, the famous school in the boys' paper *Hotspur*, should be called Colonial or Conk House. No longer could the editor of *Tiny Tots* start his weekly letter to the toddlers with the heading:

> To my little friends, where'er you may be
> In Great Britain or over the sea.

FINISH OF EMPIRE EXHIBITION 1938. *Some of crowd cheer after singing "Auld Lang Syne".*

Within ten years of the closing of the Exhibition the nationalists had taken power in South Africa and the British influence in that nation was in permanent eclipse. Another ten years and the large-scale immigration of Greeks, Italians and Yugoslavs to Australia meant an inevitable weakening of the ties which bound that country to Britain. One by one, in quick succession, the African territories found for themselves Presidents and national flags. The panoply of Empire had gone, yet the Exhibition of 1938 had had one other purpose just as important as the staging of an Imperial rally.

The great show at Bellahouston had been intended to bring work to Scotland but lighter, modern, more flexible work. The war of 1939 set this notion back a generation by giving a blood transfusion to the old industries which had been on the point of extinction. Suddenly once again coal had to be mined in Lanarkshire and ships built on the Clyde and the commercial costs did not matter and would be subsidised by a Government of a nation which was fighting for its life. It would take another 30 years before Scottish heavy industry would have its second, fatal heart attack, an industry rendered unfit by a delusory prosperity.

The major achievement of Bellahouston had been to paint on a broad canvas, with diligence and no little grace, the hopeful late Thirties and the Forties that were never to be. The Empire Exhibition of 1938 was the product of much hard thought tinged with inspiration. It was worthy and just occasionally a touch solemn maybe, but it was never pompous.

A reader F. Mc. summed up the feelings of Glaswegians very cogently in a letter of 28 October to the *Glasgow Herald:* "Saying good-bye to the Exhibition is going to be like parting from a friend and it fills one with a sense of loneliness to come. This great venture has been such a noble effort, struggling bravely against the odds of crisis, the weather clerk and criticism and now the time is drawing nigh when the sound of laughter and friendly voices will be heard no more...The people of our dear country have shown a dauntless happy spirit despite dismal weather conditions and political differences...The beautiful buildings have been such inspiring friends and the camaraderie of people of all classes and creeds has, I am sure, given many of us a feeling of well-being. I do not think I have ever seen such a successful intermingling of all classes and types of people."

"The sound of laughter and friendly voices" certainly, for fun had been a key ingredient. The great undertaking conferred on a beaten, apathetic region the priceless gift of hope and it is uniquely informative about the Scotland which disappeared forever in the September of the following year. To read the *Guide to the Empire Exhibition* is to hold in one's hand a modern Pompeii.

> The leaves of brown came tumbling down
> Remember,
> That September,
> In the rain.

ALPHABETICAL NAME INDEX

A *Aberdeen*, Marchioness of, 107
Aga Khan, H.R.H. the, 112
Albert, H.R.H. the Prince Consort, 27
Alfredo (Gypsy Orchestra) 112, 117
Allan, J.R., 10
Ambrose, 116
Armstrong, Matt., 99
Arrol, Sir William, 62
Athlone, Countess of, 109
Auden, W.H., 125
Austral, Florence, 58

B *Baldwin*, Stanley, 49
Barton, Dr. A.W., 98
Beecham, Sir Thomas, 119
Benes, Eduard, 143
Bilsland, Sir Steven, 12
Black, James, Rt. Rev., 86
Bleriot, Louis, 36
Boult, Sir Adrian, 119
Boyes, Wally, 98
Bradman, Donald, 102, 103
Britten, Benjamin, 125
Brodie, Margaret, 129
Brown, Eric, M.P., 136
Brown John (Shipbuilders), 39, 62, 105
Burns, Robert, 115
Butlin, Billy, 83, 84, 89, 90

C *Campbell*, Sir Archibald, (Lord Blythswood), 28
Cantor, Eddie, 123, 124

Chamberlain, Neville, the Rt. Hon., 12, 142, 144, 145
Cochet, Henri, 102
Coia, Jack, 129, 134
Connaught, Duke and Duchess of, 36
Cook, Willie, 99
Craigmyle, Peter, 98
Crook, R.D., 50
Crum, John, 97, 100

D *Daladier*, Edouard, 144
Dall, Evelyn, 116
Dawson, Peter, 58
Diap, Waverley Mamadou, 36, 90
Dollan, Patrick, 46, 70, 95, 110, 137, 138, 153
Douglas-Hamilton, Lord David, 62

E *Eden*, Anthony, Rt. Hon., 113
Edward VIII, H.M., 40
Elgin and Kincardine, Earl of, 12, 39, 40, 53, 82, 93, 100, 107, 127, 146
Elgin and Kincardine, Countess of, 15, 48, 61, 146
Elizabeth, H.M. Queen, 14, 40, 61, 82, 144, 146
Elizabeth II, H.M. Queen, 100
Elizabeth, H.R.H. the Princess, 74
Elliott, Walter, Rt. Hon. M.P., 137

F *Fields*, Gracie, 122
Fife, Duchess of, H.R.H. Princess Louise, 28, 34, 36

157

Flaherty, Robert, 125
Flotsam and Jetsam, 124
Forde, Florrie, 124
Fox, Roy, 116
Fyffe, Will, 116

G *Gadsby*, Frank, 92
Gadsby, Leslie, 92
George V, H.M., 108
George VI, H.M., 11, 14, 42, 49, 53, 54, 59, 82
Gilbert and Sullivan, 26
Gillick, Torrance, 98
Gloucester, Duke of, H.R.H. the, 45, 86, 108
Gloucester, Duchess of, H.R.H., the, 86, 108
Gonella, Nat, 115
Graham, David, 111
Graham, Captain S.J., 45, 46
Gray, James, 48
Grierson, John, 125, 126

H *Hall*, Henry, 116
Hamilton, George, 100
Henlein, Konrad, 143
Hitler, Adolf, 142, 144
Hitchcock, Alfred, 118, 125
Horne of Slamannan, Viscount, 68
Horton, Edward, Everett, 122
House, Jack, 112, 118, 142, 144
Hylton, Jack, 84

K *Kent*, Duke of, H.R.H., 108
Kent, Duchess of, H.R.H., the, 108
Kerr, Tom, 46
Ketelby, A., 26
King, A.B., 125
Kinnaird, Lord, 70
Kreisler, Fritz, 122

L *Lamond*, Frederic, 118
Lanchester, Elsa, 122
Lane Lupino, 117

Lauder, Sir Harry, 53, 116
Laughton, Charles, 24, 122
Lavery, Sir, John, 27, 28, 56
Lee, Mary, 116
Lenglen, Suzanne, 102
Lithgow, Sir James, 12, 39, 46, 61, 70
Livingstone, David, 20, 65, 66
Lynch, Benny, 103
Lynn, Vera, 116
Lyon, Willie, 100

M *McAneny*, George, 112
MacArthur, John, 65
MacDonald, Alister, 128, 129
MacDonald, Ramsay, Rt. Hon., 128
McDougall, Roger, 118
Macfarlane, Dugald, Very Rev., 70
McKean, Charles, 129
Mackenzie, Compton, 12
MacKenzie, Alexander, 65
Macquarie, Lachlan, 65
McQueen, Finlay, 54
Mantovani, 117
Mapson, John, 97
Margaret Rose, H.R.H. the Princess, 40
Mary, H.M. Queen, 108, 109, 142, 145, 146
Mason, Billy, 117
Masaryk, Alice, 112
Masaryk, Jan, Senior, 112
Masaryk, Jan, Junior, 143
Mayer, Camille, 92, 114
Mayerl, Billy, 124
Melba, Dame Nellie, 58
Mercer, Joe, 100
Mollison, Amy, 124
Montessori, Dr. Maria, 106
Montrose, Duke of, 51
Moore, Gerald, 118
Morrison, Herbert, 118
Morrison, Mary, 54
Muir, Donald, 36
Murray, Andrew, 36

ALPHABETICAL NAME INDEX

Murrow, Ed, 112
Mussolini, Benito, 144, 145

N *Neagle*, Anna, 24, 122
Nusslein, Hans, 100
Nuffield, Lord, 44

O *Oakley*, Charles A., 39, 108, 125, 144

P *Park*, Mungo, 65
Perry, Fred, 102
Piccaver, Alfred, 118
Plaa, M., 102
Princess Royal, H.R.H. the Princess Mary, the, 108

R *Ramillon*, R. 102
Reilly, Professor C.H., 128, 133
Rhodes, Cecil, 32
Robeson, Paul, 69, 119, 120, 121
Roberton, Hugh, 118
Roberts, Jean, 46
Roosevelt, Franklin D., 154
Ross, Lancelot, 43
Rottenburg, Paul, 32
Rowse, Herbert, 64

S *Salvesen*, Captain, 130
Scott, Sir Walter, 36
Scott-Moncrieff, George, 58
Sechel, Roderick, 60, 112
Selwyn, Eric, 90
Shakespeare, William, 100

Simons, Michael, 30
Smuts, General Jan Christian, 65
Sousa, John Philip, 31
St. Dennis, Teddy, 118
Spence, Basil, 43, 148
Stack, Prunella, 62
Stewart, Sir John, 44
Stone, Lew, 115
Strauss, Billy, 99
Suppé, Franz von, 26

T *Tait*, Thomas, 44, 45, 47, 58, 113, 127, 128, 130, 131, 135, 138
Taylor, E.A. M.P., Vice-Admiral, 68
Thomson, Tommy, 98
Tilden, Bill, 102
Troise, 117
Tweedsmuir, Lord, (John Buchan), 66, 107
Twyford, Sir Harry, 111

V *Victoria*, Queen, H.M., 27, 62

W *Wallace*, William, 36
Warren, Victor D., 46
Watson, Mrs. Annie, 90
Watt, Henry, 125
Weir, Cecil, 9, 12, 39, 40, 135, 146
Wilcox, Herbert, 122
Wilhelm II, Kaiser, 31
Wilson, Archie Y. (Alan Breck), 96, 98
Wilson, Mrs. Livingstone, 66
Wood, Sir Henry, 119

Y *Yule*, Mormal, 60, 112

159